DATE			

ANAÏS NIN

In the same series:

Modern Literature Monographs

ANAÏS NIN

Bettina L. Knapp

FREDERICK UNGAR PUBLISHING CO.
NEW YORK

Copyright © 1978 by Frederick Ungar Publishing Co., Inc.
Printed in the United States of America
Design by Anita Duncan

Library of Congress Cataloging in Publication Data
Knapp, Bettina Liebowitz, 1926–

    Anaïs Nin.

    (Modern literature monograph)
    Bibliography: p.
    Includes index.
    1. Nin, Anaïs, 1903–1977—Criticism and interpre-
tation.
PS3527.I865Z75   818'.5'209   78-57692
ISBN 0-8044-2481-0

Contents

Chronology

1947   *Children of the Albatross* published.

1950   *Four-Chambered Heart* published.

1954   Publication of *A Spy in the House of Love* (Volume IV of *Cities of the Interior*).

1958   Publication of *Solar Barque*, Part I of Volume V of *Cities of the Interior*.

1959   Alan Swallow brings out *Cities of the Interior* and later works.

1961   Publication of *Seduction of the Minotaur*, Part II of Volume V of *Cities of the Interior*.

1964   Publication of *Collages*, a collection of portraits, short stories, novellas.

1966   Publication of Volume I of *Diary* (1931–34).
         Nin's reputation reaches international status. Begins lecture tour throughout the United States, speaking most frequently at universities with Women Studies and Creative Writing Programs.

1967   Essays, "On Writing." Publishes Volume II of *Diary* (1934–39).

1968   Publication of *Novel of the Future*.

1969   Publication of Volume III of *Diary* (1939–44).

1971   Publication of Volume IV of *Diary* (1944–47).

1973   Receives honorary degree of Doctor of Fine Arts from Philadelphia College of Arts.

1974   Publication of Volume V of *Diary* (1947–55). Elected to the National Institute of Arts and Letters.

1975   Publication of *A Woman Speaks: The Lectures, Seminars, and Interviews of Anaïs Nin*, edited by Evelyn J. Hinz.

1976   Publication of Volume VI of *Diary* (1955–66). Publication of *In Favor of the Sensitive Man*.

1977   Nin dies of cancer on January 14.
         Publication of *Delta of Venus, Erotica*, which Nin had agreed to write in the 1940s to earn needed money.

1978   Publication of *The Diary of Linotte* ("The Childhood Diary").

1979   Scheduled publication of Volume VII of *Diary*.

Introduction

"Proceed from the dream outward," C. G. Jung wrote. Anaïs Nin did just that. She had always believed that the dream was a source of nourishment for the creative instinct: it enriched the imagination and aided in the development and understanding of inner pulsions. The dream enabled her to interweave painting and music with the written word, and thus to convey feeling, incarnate an aesthetic, and dramatize a psychological credo.

Nin's works are quests. Her goal was to explore the woman and artist living within her. In her prose poem *House of Incest*, she probed into her fragmented psyche—the "multiplicity of selves," as she called it. She saw a parallel image of her shattered inner world in Marcel Duchamp's canvas of a fragmented body, *Nude Descending a Staircase*. Rather than yield to despair or to passivity, Nin struggled to experience the chaos within her and to understand its component parts. Like the mystic, she attempted to untie the "knots" that prevented her awareness and to encourage the consciousness she believed was vital to the development of the writer and woman.

Nin's psychological acumen, her intuitive faculties, and her heightened powers of observation allowed her to record the minutest vibrations within her psyche. Like D. H. Lawrence (about whom she wrote a pioneering interpretation, *D. H. Lawrence: An Unprofessional Study*), she underscored images, sensations, and the inner voice of her heroines to better delineate their multileveled feelings. Like Marcel Proust's character, Nin's beings forever alter in dimension, breadth, scope; they react to environment, age, and to those they encounter. In *Cities of the Interior,* one of her female protagonists exposes the intensity of her experience through her feelings, through soundings, through impressions, and through musical phrases. She was a woman, Nin wrote, "in a state of fermentation."

Another of her women is "bound" as if "impaled on the cross of puritanism," dependent on men to the point that her boyfriend is described as "her iron lung." Nin drew a veritable *comédie humaine* of females: childlike, domineering, maternal, defensive, warring. Some of her heroines are faceless and therefore playthings "among vast mirrors," others have the aspect of the personality and the image of another —a conglomeration of splintered, undeveloped, and embryonic selves. Each woman attempted to find her identity in her own way. "Does anyone know who I am?" lamented the narrator in *House of Incest.* And she replied, "I am the other face of you." In *Ladders to Fire* we meet an actress who is successful in her career but crippled with self-doubt in the workaday world. Only in the last volume of *Cities of the Interior* did Nin's heroine experience relative harmony. She understood the meaning of psychological karma: the individual's present chaotic state is a reenactment of some unresolved previous conflict. Indeed, one's relationships and activities are merely repetitions of previously unfulfilled experiences. Everyone sets a pattern in life that must be broken and reworked at certain junctures so that growth and maturation may occur.

What was important to Nin was the development of the individual's creative faculties: the balancing, integration, and understanding of these forces within. She struggled ceaselessly to make her voice heard. The road was arduous, sometimes excoriating. Yet, she succeeded because the will, the courage, and the talent were there. Today, her books are read in many languages and throughout the world. They are absorbed by young and old, male and female, by all classes of society.

Nin has helped others to grow and evolve—women in particular. She warned, however, of certain risks involved in the woman's maturation process: the danger of being caught up in extremes. Unconsciously, many women imitate men's ways; they model their own activities and ideas upon those of the opposite sex, rather than trying to probe their own inner world and discover their own seabed. In *Notes on Feminism*, Nin wrote:

I see a great deal of negativity in the Women's Liberation Movement. It is less important to attack male writers than to discover and read women writers, to attack male-dominated films than to make films by women. If the passivity of women is going to erupt like a volcano or an earthquake, it will not accomplish anything but disaster. This passivity can be converted to creative will. If it expresses itself in war, then it is an imitation of man's methods. To become a man, or like a man, is no solution.[1]

In her friendships, too, Nin was unique. "The bridge between human beings," she wrote me, "their real secret selves lead to greater reality in relationships."[2] Consciousness was of import. Integrity, understanding, and kindness were three factors present in Nin's relationships. Facades were shorn and the inner being emerged. She gave of her time, her energy, and her encouragement—of her heart to those who needed this wonderfully helping and nourishing force.

Nin faced life as she faced death: with courage, dignity, and awareness—"the cruel lucidity which comes when you are made aware of the possibility of death."[3] She entered the eternal sanctuary of the artist with the smile that was hers, with the mischievous twinkle in her eye, and with the arabesques and circular undulations of so many of her dancing heroines—always with book in hand and a glowing heart.

1

ᐧᐧᐧᐧᐧᐧᐧᐧᐧᐧᐧᐧᐧᐧᐧᐧᐧᐧᐧᐧᐧᐧᐧᐧᐧᐧᐧᐧᐧᐧᐧ

The Diary:
"A Woman's Journey
of Self-Discovery"

The Diary of Anaïs Nin is a quest: "a woman's journey of self-discovery." Henry Miller places it "beside the revelations of St. Augustine, Petronius, Abélard, Rousseau, Proust." Authenticity, fearlessness, and artistry mark its pages. It has many levels: it is of psychological import because it analyzes inner scapes (dreams, reveries, motivations) and a variety of approaches to the unconscious; it is of aesthetic significance because it introduces readers to the world of the novelist, poet, musician, and painter; and it is of historical interest in that it reports and deals with events chronologically.

The Diary spans a lifetime and is confessional, although one must always bear in mind that it is an edited version of the original. We learn about Nin's early years in Paris (her birthplace) and the glamorous life she led with her family. With her father, Joaquin Nin, a Spanish composer and concert pianist, with her French-Danish mother, Rosa Culmell, and with her two younger brothers, Thorwald and Joaquin, she travels throughout Europe, concertgoing and meeting influential and fascinating people. This thrilling period ends abruptly in 1913 when Nin's father deserts the family. Loneliness and a sense of harrowing loss ensue. Unable to find someone in whom she can confide and deprived of the one she loves most, Nin begins her diary. It serves "to make the absent present, the ideal real." She carries it wherever she goes. It comforts her during moments of despair and helps her face the "hostile" world.

Mother and children leave Paris in 1914 and settle in New York City. Nin is sent to a parochial school but soon rebels against its constricting atmosphere. She then goes on to a high school from which she drops out. She experiences months and years of humiliation as a result of her mother's attempt to support the family by renting out rooms in their West Side home. Her inner life is rich, her fantasy world active. She is drawn to the arts: to literature, painting, and music. She learns Spanish dances from her mother's Cuban relatives and friends who visit New York.

Nin is beautiful: regal and slender with an oval face, almond-shaped eyes that are haunting yet provocative, clear white skin and wavy brown hair. Important too is her personality, which generates warmth and tenderness. Her sensitive ways, her humor, her provocative and teasing manner are factors that are forever drawing people to her. They seek her out, relate to her, confide in her.

Nin's aunt invites her to Havana, Cuba. There, on March 3, 1923, Nin marries Hugh P. Guiler, banker and financial consultant, later known as engraver and film maker under the name of Ian Hugo. In December, 1924, Nin and her husband return to Paris, where she begins to pursue a career in creative writing: *Waste of Timelessness*, a series of vignette-novellas, details Paris life with its cafés, theaters, artists, and visionaries. Her writing is precise, imagistic, and sensitive. Her friends encourage her along these lines.

In 1931, with her husband, mother, and brothers, Nin moves to Louveciennes, a spacious old house at the outskirts of Paris. Soon after, she befriends Henry Miller and his wife, June. Nin is aware of the fact that her lengthy conversations with Miller, the expatriate, serve to form and sharpen her own credo as an artist and deepen her feelings as a woman. Miller represents the realistic approach to literature. "If he annotates enough facts," writes Nin, he believes "he will finally possess the truth." As for June, she "eats and drinks symbols. Henry has no use for symbols. He eats bread, not wafers." Nin's creative world is closed to Miller.

Her domain "is the oblique, indirect world of subtle emotions and ecstasies, those which do not take a physical form, a plain physical act." Realism "cannot seize" everything, she maintains, poetry can. Nin criticizes Miller's rigidity, his naturalism, his extreme reaction to American puritanism—a tradition that makes people afraid to shed their masks and express their feelings and makes them stifle impulses beneath a heap of details and other deterministic devices.

D. H. Lawrence and Marcel Proust make powerful inroads into Nin's literary development: Lawrence's sensuality, primitive mysticism, animism, and the intensity of his feelings; Proust's "microscopic analyses," the mystery surrounding his characters as they reveal aspects of their multiple selves. Nin's growing fascination with fragmented personalities and their image equivalents, shattered mirrors, draws her to the Cubist fold—to Picasso and Braque. Their canvases reveal dismembered human bodies drawn in cubes, spheres, and triangles. These are visual replications of psychic disparities. André Breton, the father of Surrealism, and his poetic and artistic innovations fascinate her. Dreams, automatic writing, archetypal images all become food for Nin. But like Paul Valéry, she remains discerning because for her, all material emanating from the unconscious does not constitute a work of art. "I believe in impulses and naturalness, but followed by discipline in the cutting." The artist must evaluate, differentiate, divine what is of eternal value.

Nin's growing awareness of her own problems—namely, her sense of solitude and worthlessness following her father's desertion—leads to a gaping void in her life. As questions concerning a split in her psyche become more pressing and her role as an artist grows more complex, she decides to consult the psychiatrist René Allendy, author of *Problem of Destiny: Study of Inner Fatality*. He believes that individuals can control their destinies, insofar as they become aware of the unconscious tropisms inhabiting their inner world, and that they can understand these pulsations and order them about in positive ways. Nin's lack of faith in her mental and physical self he attributes to a great extent to her father's egotistical and adolescent ways. When, for example, she had been very sick with typhoid as a child, her father had said to her, "Now you are ugly. How ugly you are." As a protective device and to achieve some semblance of independence, Dr. Allendy suggests she had learned to withdraw into her own fantasy world. There she felt safe and could live out her dreams and yearnings. Through psychotherapy Nin also learns that her Don Juan father really knew nothing about women; that he viewed them through his own eyes rather than experiencing them on their terms; and that his psyche was undeveloped. For him, love consisted of a series of projections upon others of unconscious aspects of himself. Thus his attractions were narcissistic and psychologically incestuous. Dr. Allendy encourages Nin to begin writing a prose poem, which she titles *House of Incest*.

In time, Dr. Allendy's scientific approach leads to an impasse. His probings, like the deft instrument of a surgeon, help her to see "beyond the ego"; but his reductive method does not deepen her understanding of her artistic nature. He does not believe in mystery, in the unknown, or in the power of the imagination, factors vital to Nin as a writer. She decides to consult Dr. Otto Rank, author of *Myth of the Birth of the Hero* and *The Trauma of Birth*. He is a psychoanalyst whose interest centers around dreams, myths, and the creative instinct.

A Freudian apostate, Dr. Rank does not attempt to reduce everyone to a norm; rather, he seeks to "adapt each person to his own kind of universe." Phrases such as "I am an orphan" and "I am jealous," which come up in their conversations or in Nin's *Diary*, are not recognition of the motivating factors, he explains; such statements are an attempt on her part to *create herself*. "You did not want human parents," he maintains. Dr. Rank also introduces Nin, psychologically, to a notion she had experienced aesthetically in the works of D. H. Lawrence: that she exists as a woman and not as a "mirror image of man's universe. A woman should not try to emulate man, thus taking on masculine traits, she should develop herself, realize herself, gain direct vision into her own being." Otherwise she remains "what man invented."

Nin's friendships expand her vision. There is Antonin Artaud, the founder of the Theater of Cruelty and, in many regards, the seminal force behind the Theater of the Absurd. His emotional and mental ailments, searing always like glowing embers, are instrumental in his theatrical innovations: the establishment of a visceral approach to the theatrical experience. Her other friends are the sculptor Ossip Zadkine, who projects his anxieties onto his "truncated undecagonal figures in veined and vulnerable woods"; Bernard Steele, the publisher of Rank's *Don Juan and His Double*; Antonio Francisco Moralles, her dancing teacher; and Joseph Delteil, the poet and novelist who fuses detailed realism and lyrical qualities in his work.

A turning point in Nin's life comes in 1934. She gives birth to a stillborn baby. As a result of this traumatic experience, she, who had rejected Catholicism, never to return to it, discovers the real meaning of God—not in the ossified concepts of organized religion, but in her personal and transcendental rapport with Deity. "An immense joy and a sense of the greatness of life, eternity" fills her being. She knows now the meaning of birth and rebirth. "I was born. I was born woman. . . . This joy which I found in the love of man, in creation, was completed by communion with God."

When Rank decides to practice psychotherapy in New York in 1934, he asks Nin to join him and help him in his practice, and she accepts. She takes rooms at the "Hotel Chaotica" (as she refers to her living quarters in Volume II of her *Diary*), the name symbolizing city life: "all external, all action, no thought, no meditation, no dreaming, no reflection, only the exuberance of action." The change of tempo and atmosphere that she is experiencing in New York alienates her. Rank's approach to psychotherapy, she subsumes, harmonizes with the pace of the new world: to take hold of the patient's present conflict, attack it then, by "a quick-moving progression from the present conflict," analyze and cure it.

Nin concentrates her energies on her work. She becomes "an archaeologist of the soul." However, her approach to analysis is not scientific; it is poetic. She avoids clinical language. As a writer, she knows that language has "power," and therefore she chooses her words with care. She also takes time to describe character, motivations, and feelings to her patients. She does not want them to feel like objects, numbers, or classifications. The warmth she generates and the empathy she arouses in the psychologically ill make her a gifted healer of souls.

Despite her thriving practice, Nin remains unfulfilled as an artist. She realizes now that her contribution to society can never be made as a therapist, only as an artist. Important, too, is the fact that the close bonds she has built up with her patients during the course of the therapeutic hours prevent her from living a life of her own. Their loves and traumas keep intruding upon her world. She decides to return to Paris.

The months spent in New York, however, have not been lost. Her understanding of people and of herself has deepened. Her many new acquaintances and friends have broadened her outlook. She has met Theodore Dreiser, whom she respects as a writer but "who does not believe in the soul"; Waldo Frank, whom she describes as "warm, human . . ." a "man who did not harden or die." She was also to meet the brilliant and hospitable Rebecca West, Norman Bel Geddes, Raymond Massey, and John Huston. Nin's admiration for Djuna Barnes is expressed in a letter to her: "I have to tell you of the great, deep beauty of your *Nightwood*. . . . A woman rarely writes as a woman, as she feels, but you have."

In Paris again, Nin feels like "an adventurer, a nomad

. . . I feel no boundaries within myself, no walls, no fears." Filled with inner strength, she can find her way alone and function as an artist. She rents a houseboat on the Seine and lives out her love affair with Gonzalo, a Peruvian musician and revolutionary. This affair she later fictionalizes in her novel *Four-Chambered Heart*. It is through him that her own political notions are sharpened. With the outbreak of the Spanish Civil War, Gonzalo refuses to remain detached. A proponent of Marxist dialectics, he seeks involvement in the conflagration, but his courage remains at the talking level; passivity takes over. Nin is apolitical. She believes in the cause of the loyalists, but "I am not committed to any of the political movements, which I find full of fanaticism and injustice, but in the face of every human being, I act democratically and humanely." Society as a whole cannot benefit from revolution: "The Inquisition tortured human beings who did not believe in Catholicism, and . . . this revolution will torture and is torturing all those who do not adhere fanatically to it." Someday, she continues, "these downtrodden workmen will become the tyrants, the same greedy inhuman bosses."

Meanwhile, old friendships are maintained and new ones made. Nin encourages Miller to publish his *Tropic of Cancer* and writes a "Preface" for it. She visits the sculptor Constantin Brancusi, whose "Bird Without Wings" she describes as "One long lyrical flight, piercing space." New friends include: Chana Orloff, whose sculptures express the power embedded within the artist's soul; Jules Supervielle, "a haunted man with human roots"; and Lawrence Durrell, with whom "I had instant communication." André Breton disappoints her. "I expected he would be poetically and sensitively alert to the atmosphere of my life, to my inarticulate intuitions. He was intellectual. He talked about ideas, not impressions or sensations."

Her visits to Morocco make her experience that land as a living corpus, a mirror image of her own inner realm: she

steps "into the labyrinth of their streets, streets like intes-
tines, two yards wide, into the abyss of their dark eyes, into
peace."

Pain encroaches on Nin's life. At her father's "thou-
sandth concert in Paris," which she attends, she sees him
slump over on the piano. Although he does not die from the
stroke he has suffered, the life of love affairs, adulations, and
luxury is ended—and he decides to return to Cuba where the
Nin family now lives. Nin is overcome with pity, not with
guilt. "He was fulfilling his destiny," she writes. During his
life "he had sought only his own pleasure, and made no
sacrifice for anyone." But after his departure, she realizes
that her love,

which had died a thousand times, and been buried, was reawak-
ened intact. Does love ever die, I asked. For years I buried it. I
buried it in a novel. . . . I buried it under other loves. I looked at
him without illusion. Yet when he left . . . I wept for him, and
awakened in the morning thinking of him. I never know death
or indifference. Time kills nothing in me, even though I tried to
deliver myself of all possession through art.

In 1939 at the outbreak of World War II, Nin leaves
Paris for New York because she realizes that the life she has
known is over. "I felt every cell and cord which tied me to
France snapping in me, the parting from a pattern of life I
loved, from an atmosphere rich, creative and human, from
intimacy with people and a city." In New York she feels like
a "displaced person," an alien. Feelings of independence are
followed by periods of guilt. The idea that she has abandoned her friends in France less fortunate than she, "to an
unknown fate," corrodes her soul. But Nin is not one to
indulge in negativity; her imagination, sensibility, and thirst
for the creative life sustain her during her moments of
despair.

Nin moves to Greenwich Village where she develops a
circle of friends: Frances Steloff, of the Gotham Book Mart;
Dorothy Norman, who publishes Nin's story "Birth" in the

magazine *Twice a Year*; Yves Tanguy, who loves "to paint
bleached bones lying dead in the sun of emptiness"; Paul
Rosenfeld, the critic; Sherwood Anderson, who looks "like a
doctor, a businessman, a banker"; Salvador Dali, that "great
indisputable genius," whose wife manipulates everything and
everyone for her husband; Luise Rainer, the actress whom
Nin describes as wearing a "long, white, floating dress, her
hair floating, her gestures light and graceful . . . a mobile,
fluid quality and radiance" and whose unhappy marriage to
Clifford Odets nearly destroys her; Edgar Varèse, the "im-
posing . . . tall, rough-hewn . . . fierce, revolutionary" who
teases Nin because of her admiration for Proust and tells her
she suffers from a disease called *Proustatite*; Yanko Varda,
the Hungarian artist "who delivers us from the stranglehold
of realism, the lack of passion and wit of other painters" and
who "fulfills the main role of the artist, which is to transform ugliness into beauty"; Canada Lee, the star of *Native
Son*, whose warm voice Nin calls "orange-toned"; Jacques
Lipschitz, "all intellectual, abstractions, theories"; Leonora
Carrington, artist and writer was concerned because "the
sources of her images in painting and the source of her
material in writing might run dry. . . ."

Economic problems beset Nin, and she is unable to pay
her phone bill or buy clothes. Thus she agrees to write
erotica to earn needed money. (Eventually these stories are
published in a volume entitled *Delta of Venus, Erotica*.)
Nin persists in writing her short stories and novels despite
the fact that publishers keep turning them down. She realizes
that although she is talented she will not become a popular
or accepted writer. Unlike Steinbeck, Hemingway, Miller, or
Wolfe, who depict outer reality, her world is expressed
through undercurrents, sensations, and tropisms that arise
within her, images and symbols gathered from her dreams
that she interprets from a mythological and eternal point of
view.

After Gonzalo's arrival in New York, Nin borrows $75
from Frances Steloff and $100 from other friends. She then

buys an old-fashioned printing press and rents a loft at 144 MacDougal Street, where she and Gonzalo cut paper and set type. "We dreamt, ate, talked, slept with the press." She prints her short novel *Winter of Artifice* with Ian Hugo's line engravings and experiences a sense of joy and fulfillment at its completion. The printing of *Under a Glass Bell*, a collection of thirteen short stories (which include "Houseboat," "The Mouse," "Birth") that are among the best of Nin's fictional works, also excites her. Each of the stories is of gem quality: cut for beauty of form and polished for texture, color, and brilliance. Edmund Wilson's favorable review in the *New Yorker*, photographs of Nin in the magazine *Town and Country*, telephone calls and letters finally gain recognition for the unknown writer. The first printing of *Under a Glass Bell* sells out in three weeks.

Nin and Gonzalo now begin to attract the attention of other authors as well as the engraver William Hayter. The press is moved into larger quarters. Nin completes her novel *Ladders to Fire*, which is accepted by Dutton. *The New York Times* calls it "A Surrealist Soap Opera." Diana Trilling's cerebrality and apparent limited vision cause her to criticize Nin's writing quite ruthlessly: for example, she judges the heroine Stella, in "This Hunger," (the first part of *Ladders to Fire*), as not real. "We never see her going to the icebox for a snack," writes Mrs. Trilling. Although Edmund Wilson considers Nin's books more significant than those of Marquand or Isherwood, because hers "explore a new realm of material . . . a new feminine point of view," Nin cannot find a publisher for her future novels.

Her feelings of rejection and inadequacy are so strong that Nin reevaluates her approach to psychiatry. Since life is a growing and ever-fluid process, there are periods during a person's life when analysis is in order; but there are also other periods when assimilation of the findings must take place. She compares analysis to medicine. "When I gained my orientation, I turned my back on analysis, and went back to living, to writing." Analysis must help people to live, enjoy, and find fulfillment. It should not be a crutch nor an escape mechanism. "The inner chambers of the soul are like the photographer's darkroom. Like a laboratory. One cannot stay there all the time or it becomes the solitary cell of the neurotic." Esther Harding, the Jungian therapist, explains to Nin the necessity of integrating the *shadow* (those unconscious contents that people consider negative but are not necessarily that) into the whole personality. Dr. Harding also emphasizes the necessity of understanding the various *personae* (masks) one wears during social confrontations and the dangers involved if overidentification with them occurs: a split personality and alienation from reality.

Nin is drawn to the story of Caspar Hauser, she writes, because she considers it more "beautiful than that of Christ." It tells of a "dreamer destroyed by the world." She identifies with Caspar, who could not survive the coldness and calculating nature of people. Artists too, if unappreciated, feel the deep hurt that comes with public and commercial rejection, with misunderstanding and distrust.

Attracted to youth at this juncture in her life, Nin understands the needs, wants, and problems of young people. For many, she represents the positive mother principle and becomes the harbinger of strength, understanding, and love. Because of her constructive attitude, many young people find renewal through her, a lust for life, a harmony of the soul—and Nin is encouraged. She embarks on lecture tours at universities, poetry centers, and clubs throughout the United States. Her direct contact with the emotional crises, rebellions, exaltations, and passions of the young enable her to respond to their needs in lectures.

The liberation of France in 1944 brings "JOY, JOY, JOY, JOY." For days Nin is incapable of work. Travel is on the agenda now. Nin goes west, then on to Mexico for some months. "The air inhaled was like a drug of forgetfulness." Each moment is enjoyed for itself. "The colors of the sea, the sailboats, the flowers, and the papaya on the table . . . The festivities of nature anesthetized all thoughts of sorrow."

Upon her return to New York, Nin pursues her writing of fiction and nonfiction. In her essay "Realism and Reality," she expresses her antirealistic, antinaturalistic, and antiexpressionistic credo with pith and point. She is not interested in Steinbeck's or Hemingway's "vulgar" and "violent" approach to society. She prefers the stilling of life's fluid and living moments through the image as practiced by Proust's "microscopic" analyses and Joyce's "undifferentiated flow of associations." Of import to the artist, she maintains, is to discover his own creative elements and to synthesize, structure, and articulate these in viable and concrete forms.

Nin is still beset by difficulties involving the publication of her works. She meets the analyst Dr. Inge Bogner, who "seemed to fuse two qualities: acuity with sympathy." Dr. Bogner understands the artistic temperament and the anguish when poor criticism follows the publication of a work. Nin believes that if the artist has sufficient faith in his talents, he must stand firm. The artist is a *hero*, in André Malraux's sense of the word. To accept such a notion intellectually—that is, to admit that courage and strength are needed to face the castigations of the critics, is relatively simple; but to assimilate such premises emotionally is another question. It is mainly in this domain that Nin works with Dr. Bogner. And she is strengthened for the next hurt —the rejection of *A Spy in the House of Love* by Houghton-Mifflin, Doubleday, Scribner, and other publishers. Nin knows that many artists have experienced similar destinies. When the painter Rousseau was asked "Why did you place a sofa in the middle of a jungle?" he simply answered, "One has the right to paint one's dreams."

Nin travels more extensively and finds renewal in California, New Mexico, and Mexico. Plunging into nature, she nourishes her being and reactivates her instinct: "I feel a new woman would be born there." Contact between her inner and outer worlds has created a new dynamism; it has increased her strength and confidence in herself and her goals. The feelings of torment and anguish (suffocation, being "torn apart") give way to inner peace, calm, and detachment. She no longer feels impelled to go to France or to have her works published. "I only need to continue my personal life, so beautiful and in full bloom, and to do my major work, which is the *Diary*. I merely forgot for a few years what I had set out to do."

When in 1949 her personal belongings and furniture arrive in New York from Louveciennes, she realizes that the objects she had once treasured are no longer meaningful to her. They belong to a romantic life she had led a long time ago on a houseboat on the Seine; they belong to adolescence. She had catalogued all of these objects in her *Diary* and described them in *Under a Glass Bell*. Objects "die when they are no longer illuminated by certain experiences and heightened moments of one's life. My attachment to them died, and they lost their glow as soon as I stopped loving them." They have become "wreckage from a great emotional journey."

With her father's death in Cuba (October, 1949) and her mother's death in California (August, 1954), Nin's thoughts begin to center on death. She wants to assess its meaning in terms of her own psyche and spirituality. She believes in "the disintegration of the body" but cannot accept the notion that all she has "learned, experienced, accumulated" could vanish and be wasted. "Like a river, it must flow somewhere. Proust's life flowed into me, became part of my life. His thoughts, his discoveries, his visions each year visit me, each year bring me deeper messages. There must be continuity."

It is the year 1955. Nin, who leans heavily on her unconscious to lead the way in the workaday world, decides that she will publish her *Diary* after she has a dream that began: "I opened my front door and was struck by mortal radiation." In revealing her innermost thoughts, she is ready to accept hostility from critics and feels strong enough to withstand the ridicule and the hurt of an unfeeling public. Readers would certainly label her neurotic and narcissistic, as they had labeled André Gide, Julien Green, Virginia Woolf, and countless other authors of journals and diaries.

I had faith in the *Diary*. I had put my most natural, most truthful writing in it. I was weary of secrecy, of showing only a small portion of my work. I felt the strongest and best of my work was there. I felt a maturity in the editing. I felt able to solve the problems.

Her course is set: "I had to act according to my own nature or else the *Diary* itself would be destroyed." The preparation of the *Diary* for publication would be difficult and time consuming; also a labor of love.

Nin's life is full. It is exciting. *Collages*, a collection of portraits, short stories, and novellas, is published in 1964. Henry Miller writes: "The book abounds in magical descriptions of a highly original and sensuous nature. The best of collages fall apart with time; these will not." And in the *Times Literary Supplement*, she reads: "A handful of perfectly told fables, and prose which is so daringly elaborate, so accurately timed . . . using words as magnificently colorful, evocative and imagistic as any plastic combination on canvas but as mysteriously idiosyncratic as any abstract." In *The Novel of the Future*, Nin studies the evolution and the techniques of the poetic novel and advocates Jung's dictum: "Proceed from the dream outward." The publication in Italian and Dutch of *Under a Glass Bell* and in Dutch of *Ladders to Fire*, invitations to lecture in Sweden, France, Japan, and throughout the United States bolster Nin's faith in herself. But commercial publishers are still rejecting her works. Alan Swallow, a poet himself and a man of integrity who publishes only what he loves and at a small profit, decides to print Nin's fiction. He "protects minority writers" and "enriches the majority."

The question still remains as to who would publish the *Diary*. Gunther Stuhlmann has edited Volume I and tries to place it in a large publishing house. Rejections are his answer—not commercially viable, not sufficiently intellectual, not credible, not popular. At last, Hiram Haydn of Harcourt, Brace reacts differently. He has the courage of his convictions: "I love it. I will do it."

Joy is followed by pain. Sickness imposes itself on Nin. Although she has had many bouts with pneumonia, this time her illness—cancer—is more serious and surgery is required. She feels like Proust, who hoped he would be able to finish his work before death intruded. Nin's convalescence is long.

Volume I of her *Diaries* is published in 1966. Reviews, public appearances, television programs, and celebrations follow. Nin writes: "It is my thousand years of womanhood I am recording, a thousand women."

During the following years, the next five volumes of Nin's *Diaries* are published. More lecture tours, travel to the Far East and to Europe, and the deepening of friendships allow Nin to experience warm feelings of fulfillment.

But then, cancer recurs. This time several lengthy and dangerous operations are necessary. Despite the excruciating pain, Nin's spirit is positive and her soul serene. She expresses her feelings in a letter to me on May 28, 1976:

I am glad that my illness gives me so much time to read. I can only work 4 or 5 pages a day to finish volume 7 [the last volume of the *Diaries*].

About my health it is hard to explain. . . . I can't imagine a worse illness for my active temperament. Fortunately I can work, read, take walks.

Aside from my health it has been a year of rewards, honors, doctorates, homages and letters from all over the world, and interesting visitors.

Anaïs Nin does not complete Volume VII of her *Diaries*. She dies on January 14, 1977.

2

∽∾∽∾∽∾∽∾∽∾∽∾∽∾∽∾∽∾∽∾∽∾∽∾∽∾∽∾

Creative Criticism—
D. H. Lawrence:
An Unprofessional Study

"They who are to be judges must also be performers," Aristotle wrote in *Politics*. Nin was both: critic and writer of fiction. Her approach to literature was creative; her analyses and evaluation of works under scrutiny fused subjective and objective reactions as well as individual and collective ideations. *D. H. Lawrence: An Unprofessional Study,* her first published work, is an aesthetic, visceral, and spiritual experience. Within the pages exist clusters of insights, themes, stylistic devices, philosophical and metaphysical probings that she will flesh out in her later works.

Nin rejected the systems and formulas of conventional criticism with their cerebral approach to art and life. She unleashed her moorings and cut ties with what was. But her rebellion against the status quo did not imply aimless wanderings or a negative attitude. On the contrary, her uprooting paved the way for a rerouting and rerooting into steadier and more solid ground. It took the form of a *sinking into self*, an *inner contemplation*.

Unlike critics such as Jean François Marmontel, who drew a cut-and-dry line between beauty as it existed in nature and beauty inherent in the work of art; or l'Abbé Dubos, who suggested that beauty exists in the eye of the beholder and was a question of personal taste; or Charles Lamb, Henry Hazlitt, and Charles Augustin Sainte-Beuve, who considered themselves repositories for collective opinions, Nin's way was subdued and modest. It entailed an inner trajectory fired by the excitement of self-discovery.

An enemy of naturalism, positivism, rationalism, and scientism—which Nin felt distorted reality and constricted the imagination—her approach to literature resembled Lawrence's as delineated in his *Studies in Classic American Literature*. Of importance to Nin and Lawrence were the catalytic effect of images, symbols, and sensations, the musicality and density of the prose and its impact on the reader's imagination. *D. H. Lawrence: An Unprofessional Study* therefore differs from the standard well-documented and well-argued critical work in that it is neither a composite of statistics, facts, and groupings of structures and themes, nor is it didactic or pontifical. Instead, aggregations of eidetic images, metaphors, and symbols are offered the reader, each perceived internally and relationally; each endowed with the energy to penetrate the heart of the poetic mystery.

Nin searched to understand the particular works under study and her relationship to them. To understand did not imply cognition alone; it included visceral knowledge. One without the other represented a divided human being, an incomplete study, a half-hearted attempt. She linked what Pythagoras referred to as body (*soma*) and soul (*psyche*). In her hands, literature became a quest to discover the secrets associated with the artistic process and, thus, the increasing of consciousness. As Nin probed into the essence of Lawrence's creative world, a wealth of images, symbols, and intuitions flowed forth; geological folds, heretofore enclosed in darkness, were illumined. Slowly an inner architecture became visible: Lawrence's soul and by extension, Nin's. To know Lawrence as Nin felt him is to be infused with his lifeblood—his creative impulse and hers. In this sense, Nin was a trailblazer: one who showed the way to greater riches and profounder realms.

As the title indicates, *D. H. Lawrence: An Unprofessional Study* is dual in nature. It is "unprofessional," and

therefore it violates the codes and ethics of the critic's pro-
fession. It is also a "study" and because of this, Nin applied
mental faculties to the acquisition of knowledge. In her essay
she projected her unconscious world into Lawrence's universe and via a symbiotic relationship, transforming her
personal vision into the collective sphere, experienced the
mysteries embedded in his writings. The "universality of
the subjective experience," as Kant phrased it in *Analytic
of the Beautiful*,[1] allows a welding of personalities: Nin as
critic and creative artist and Lawrence as the object of her
scrutiny.

Nin's course was intuitive, not intellectual. To follow
her into the intricacies of Lawrence's style—into those
depths of his characters, the harmonies and cacophonies of
his inner and outer scapes—is to take a fantastic voyage: to
"flow forward" with the creatures of his fantasy and to
follow their feelings as manifested in impulses and gestures.
Nin used a variety of techniques to chart her course: synesthesia, which opens the world of the senses; the dream,
which allowed her to peer into the unconscious and delineate in sharply focused images the colorful, subdued tonalities
of shapes that emerge full-blown, only to blend back into
shadows in the objective psyche; symbols, which enabled her
to express the inexpressible, to call the unknown into existence.

Intuition

Intuition, as Henri Bergson suggested, is a direct and
instantaneous way of knowing. The experience involves the
entire being, "primal consciousness," as Nin called it, "pre-
mental" activity that has "nothing to do with cognition" (p.
2). The intuitive approach to literature encouraged Nin to
sink into a text and contemplate it as one does geological
strata. As she plunged into the mysterious sphere that
opened to her, it became the source of her creative élan. In
these new spiritual-physical climes, the multiple fused with

the one, space with spacelessness, time with timelessness; the "unmoved mover" (to use Aristotle's wording) was sensed and nonhuman knowledge absorbed. Mystics, from St. Augustine to Abraham Abulafia, have described such intuitive experiences as a face-to-face encounter with God. For Nin, intuition implied a confrontation with that transpersonal force that lived inchoate within her every fiber—that gave sustenance, that nurtured life.

Intuition places the individual "within an object," Bergson wrote in *An Introduction to Metaphysics* (1903), thus it allows the individual to become aware of what is unique and, therefore, inexpressible in the work. Analytical methods describe the object from the outside; they portray its features from a variety of perspectives. But then, Nin suggested, only the shell or the husk is visible. Intuition penetrates the object under study like a laser beam; it allows for heightened vision.

"Intuitional reasoning," Nin wrote, enabled her to experience the inner architecture of Lawrence's beings and to combine the visceral with the cognitive. Lawrence's "dark dogs" were encountered as they existed inchoate in all of his characters, no longer hidden and repressed but burgeoning and awakening to life's variegated experiences. Instincts, Nin declared, should not be reviled. They possess their own wisdom. They transcend the thinking function, which Nin described as "an adroit juggler who can make everything balance and fall right" (p. 8). Sophists and casuists can argue any point and make it seem valid. Instincts do not lie. To know people *plain* is to listen to the "body" to learn its "dreams" and its "needs."

We are at opposite poles of Plato and the Christian ethic and aesthetics, which considered the intellect the divine part of man and taught the subjugation of the senses—as Nin described it, the eradication of "the livingness of the body" (p. 9). Lawrence, and Nietzsche before him, considered the post-Socratic Christian ethic as the destroyer of the body, man's vital nature, and the builder of the mind that had become with time a hollow instrument: the Apollonian at the expense of the Dionysian way. Lawrence's denunciation of the Christian ethos did not imply an atheistic view. On the contrary, Lawrence was "true to his deep instinctive sense of religion," Nin wrote (p. 39). He experienced God in a personal and powerful manner.

Lawrence experienced the sacred in life and not the God of the intellect, not the ethical, pure, sinless deity whose moral dictates organized religion had interpreted as a rejection of the flesh. Lawrence's God was an energetic force that allowed the individual a communion of body and spirit, thus contact with life's flow.

Both Lawrence and Nin discarded the taboos organized religion had superimposed upon individuals and societies: an ossification of what had once been a living, vibrant symbol and had become a guarantee against fear. Lawrence's and Nin's world embraced the universe as viewed in the self, a composite of opposites—the mystic's All. Like Emerson, the New England transcendentalist, they rejected external authority and placed their confidence in an inner light. For all three, religion was "the same wine poured into different glasses."

The unification of polarities, such as body and soul or good and evil, entails a "vitalistic" struggle that Lawrence and Nin associated with the life force—with blood as it pulsates in powerful rhythms, reflecting and deflecting the meanderings within the individual and the collective. In *The Plumed Serpent*, Lawrence rejected the Christian Church and chose instead the old, still powerful and still mysterious gods. They activated his senses and his imagination. Man's relationship with divinity is described in this novel as an initiation leading directly into the ecstatic experience, during the course of which the unknown and the ephemeral are transformed into the actual and eternal—the crude sensation is transformed into the polished work of art. Lawrence's God, who "is nameless and unknowable,"[2] makes the fusion of man with deity possible. Deity manifests itself in many forms and ways, Lawrence suggested, many Gods "come into me and leave me again. And they have very various wills, I must say."

For Lawrence and for Emerson, God is that power which lives in the poet, that force which pulsates in the universe—that potency which makes great men. In "The Over-Soul," Emerson described this transpersonal energy as

a great public power in which he [man] can draw, by unlocking, at all risks, his human doors, and suffering the ethereal tides to roll and circulate through him; then he is caught up into the life of the universe, his speech is thunder, his thought is law, and his works are as universally intelligible as the planets and animals.

The physical without the spiritual is as inadequate as the spiritual without the physical. Only complete involvement of the two sides of man can heal the breach in the psyche and make it whole again.

Lawrence's and Nin's approach to literature and life in general involved the whole being. Senses were aroused and the creative élan functioned. And they were not alone in denouncing the westerner's emphasis on developing only the spirit and the intellect. In *Out of My Later Years*, Einstein (whom Nin mentions) looked upon the intellect as a force that blocks discovery:

And certainly we should take care not to make the intellect our god; it has, of course, powerful muscles, but no personality. It cannot lead, it can only serve; and it is not fastidious in its choice of a leader. This characteristic is reflected in the qualities of its priests, the intellectuals. The intellect has a sharp eye for methods and tools, but is blind to ends and values. So it is no wonder that this fatal blindness is handed on from old to young and today involves a whole generation.[3]

Synesthesia

Synesthesia not only was used as a literary technique by Baudelaire, Rimbaud, Mallarmé, and others, it was also a device that aided the mystic in experiencing the higher spheres. Synesthesia implies a unification of the senses: the visual may be heard, smelled, touched, and tasted or the tasted may be heard, seen, smelled, and felt, and so on. In his famous "Letter to the Seer," Rimbaud declared that the real poet (the creative being) "must be a *seer*." In ancient times the creative artist was looked upon as a seer, a being who could envision life monistically and eternally as a unit, not ephemerally in its differentiated phase. To become a seer, according to Rimbaud, one must experience life in a new way, synesthetically, then the unknown becomes actuality.

Synesthesia may be looked upon as a giant awakening, a psychic happening, a flaring up of forces within the unconscious. It enables the artist to experience simultaneity of sense impressions, to see the work of art coming into being, and to contact new languages, forgotten species, preformal life. The mystics Jakob Boehme and Isaac Luria, for instance, had known such ecstatic moments when they leaped into their inner world, discovered its treasures, and constellated these in their writings. To allow the synesthetic experience to bear its full fruit, the artist must be willing to undergo a momentary eclipse of his conscious personality, a dissociation of the ego. He then allows the powers of the collective unconscious to engulf him: the inner eye and ear feel the cadences and aromas—in Nin's words, "the bulginess of sculpture," "the heavy material fulness" expressed in rhythms as well as in "nuances of pain" (p. 78). A new creative center is discovered by the artist, an unlimited source of inspiration.

The techniques of synesthesia allowed Nin to extract new riches from Lawrence's works and taught her another way leading to the inner domain. "Lawrence's language," Nin wrote, "makes a physical impression because he projected his physical response into the thing he observed" (p. 71). A flow from her primitive self into Lawrence's activated a combustible state and set up the dynamism necessary to unshackle the floodgates, which activated vortexes and illuminated the darkened realms behind gestures, feelings, and the word. As a result of such swift sensorial interchange, the unconscious motivations of Lawrence's characters as well as his philosophical and metaphysical insights emerged for Nin not as abstract essences relegated to some remote ethereal realm, but as living forces in the life process:

He has tried many times to express the texture of different skins, the chameleonesque qualities of eyes, the sensations given by the feel of water and rain on the body, the changes in the colors of the day. His sensorial penetration is complete. That is why his most abstract thought is always deep reaching: it is really concrete, it passes through the channels of the senses. (p. 78)

Synesthesia is an energetic process. It enables the transformation of amorphous forms into substance, the idea into the act. It arouses tension and allows the flow and possible conflagration of composite sensations to catapult forth into the poetic universe. Nin's discovery of Lawrence's synesthetic approach to the spiritual and natural forces in the universe showed her the course to take to discover—after her own arduous descents—the germ of her burgeoning feelings, ideas, and visions.

The synesthetic way captures life in its flux and action in its counteraction. Nin and Lawrence, then, followed the Heraclitean doctrine: the only reality is change. The notion of permanence is an illusion, the product of sophistry, paradoxes, and casuistic reasoning. Within each entity (organic and inorganic) opposites exist: being and nonbeing; and the only true state is that of transition. If strife were ended, Heraclitus wrote, so would life.

All is in a state of flux; all spells opposition in life. Such a condition must be accepted and used to the individual's advantage. For Lawrence and Nin, activity, combustion, combinations, and recombinations were the *sine qua non* of the synesthetic—and poetic—experience. To force a reshuffling of emotion requires aggressiveness on the part of the creative individual. It pierces husks and shears off layers of conventional material, prosaic screens that hide the invisible domain. Such powerful inner activity externalizes unconscious contents and forces past experiences to impose themselves on present situations; it alters circumstances, relationships, continuity, and contiguity. The work of art feeds on kaleidoscopic sensations, and the rich nutrients it confronts pave the way for growth and development—until its autonomy is experienced.

It is not in "an upper plane, in the head, the brain," Nin stated, that such an inflow and outflow of primordial sensations and impulses can expand the poet's vision (p. 5); rather, it is in the solar plexus. There, Nin declared, one finds "blood-consciousness" that causes the creative act to manifest itself. The solar plexus functions as an inner sun (*solar*), a light that radiates in darkness and warms remote and insalubrious realms. The sun also stands for spirit and, paradoxically, for consciousness. The *plexus* consists of a network of vessels, nerves, and fibers that, when activated by solar forces, set the inner machinery into motion and commotion. When the solar plexus is touched, radiating nerve fibers take on harmony and forms. In *Sons and Lovers*, Lawrence's creatures functioned powerfully; they took root in a preformal realm, in rough and dark regions. It is here that Lawrence contacted the "source of life," the multileveled states of consciousness (p. 52). In *Fantasia of the Unconscious*, he wrote: "As the height falls and the unconscious sinks deeper, suddenly the blood is heard hoarsely calling. Suddenly the deep centers of the sexual consciousness rouse to their spontaneous activity" (p. 52).

It is not known whether Lawrence had read Freud before he wrote *Sons and Lovers*, which is frequently described as a novel dramatizing the Oedipal situation. It is known, however, that Lawrence's wife had read Freud beforehand and had discussed Freud's ideas with her husband. In later works, Lawrence openly disagreed with Freud. He did not believe that sexual impulses were the *sine qua non* in the psychological development of the individual; nor did he feel that neurotics should become consciously aware of their repressed instincts and drives. Lawrence was also against Freud's tendency to overconceptualize experience, thereby killing its mystery. Like Blake, Lawrence refused to be limited by any doctrines, even by those he invented. To allow ossification to take place, in the domain of either the senses or ideas, is to halt the dynamic life process and allow it to wither.[4]

Creativity brings the unknown into the known world, unconscious contents into consciousness, the amorphous into palpable form—it unblocks and unleashes. Such activity, whether the artist uses the synesthetic approach or other techniques, is of enormous importance to his work. For Lawrence and Nin, the élan vital was experienced. As Bergson suggested in *Creative Evolution* (1906), it enabled the work to acquire dimension and depth; it helped the artist mobilize the organic and inorganic into a vast galvanic whole. In Nin's words:

The world D. H. Lawrence created cannot be entered through the exercise of one faculty alone: there must be a threefold desire of intellect, of imagination, and of physical feeling, because he erected his world on a fusion of concepts, on a philosophy that was against division, on a plea for a whole vision: "to see with the soul and the body." For the world he takes us into is shadowed, intricate. It is "ultimately chaos, lit up by visions, or not lit up by visions." (p. 1)

The Dream

In Lawrence's works "dreams and reality are often interwoven," Nin wrote, "just as they are in our own natures" (p. 26). Because dreams and reality are frequently blended, polarities fuse, the nonmaterial acquires materiality. It was within the dream world that Nin experienced the creatures of Lawrence's fantasy, first viscerally, then slowly articulat-

ing her discoveries in a series of perceptions and appercep-
tions.

Nin felt that Lawrence's characters were not built in
the conventional sense. They did not evolve or grow according to well-planned plots and situations. They emerged instead chaotically from the collective unconscious, where the
archetypal dream takes root. When Lawrence wrote of his
admiration for Balzac, "a magnificent and supreme"[5] writer,
it was not Balzac's realism he lauded, the emphasis he placed
on detail and decor. It was Balzac the mystic who fascinated
Lawrence: Balzac the creative artist who united the disparate and linked outer and inner environments when molding
his characters. Lawrence's phantasms in *Women in Love*
and in *Sons and Lovers* emerged from his subliminal depths,
virile beings who pulsated with life and expressed themselves
in emotional patterns.

The dream is unrestricted in its aesthetic and moral
limitations. Therefore Lawrence's creatures, who were mod-
eled in part from dreams, experience their multiple sensations freely, not hedonistically, in a deepening vision of life,
gaining increased awareness and consciousness into self and
by extension the cosmos. Like Cézanne, to whom Lawrence
alluded,[6] he shaped and reshaped, molded and remolded the
stuff from which his novels were made, perhaps not in triangles, cylinders, and cones but, within his own frame of
reference, in blazing or dimming lights, in swelling or dis-
solving forms. Like Cézanne, Lawrence seized life in its
fluidity; color and feeling tones were articulated in tactile
reverberations, in silent dialogues—the soul groping to express itself.

To use the dream as a literary vehicle requires a turning
inward, Nin suggested, a guiding of life's flow of energy into
the psyche. Such a condition entails isolation. During certain
stages in the creative process, writers must cut themselves off
from society. If a depth experience is to be conveyed and a
new ontology delineated, fresh centers of feeling must be
discovered; therefore, writing has "to be accomplished in

loneliness and isolation." To know solitude is certainly no new concept in the creative field. The artist has been crying about his loneliness and lamenting his isolation for centuries. However, isolation has its positive side. For mystics, such as Boehme and Blake, and for writers, such as Lawrence, isolation weeds out draining forces, Nin explained; it allows the seed, the idea, and the feeling to benefit fully from the nutrients needed for the growth process. But solitude as lived by Lawrence in no way implied a Trappist's existence. Lawrence knew a long and profound relationship with his wife. He traveled extensively, each time enriching himself through fresh climes and outer scapes. In his essay "Edgar Allan Poe," Lawrence referred to the type of isolation that allows the artist to absorb the deep rich soil of his inner system and to understand impulse/sensation, which is the road leading to self-knowledge.

The dream allowed Lawrence that isolation necessary to enter into communication with the forces within his unconscious and experience their arcana—the mystery of his genius. Nin wrote:

Imprisoned in our flesh lives the body's own genie, which Lawrence set out to liberate. He found that the body had its own dreams, and that by listening attentively to these dreams, by surrendering to them, the genie can be evoked and made apparent and potent. (p. 10)

Nin suggested that there is a way of recording dreams; but not in the manner of some modern writers who insert into their works the dream's "triteness." In such novels the "dream has dwindled" into sequences of "pitiful, graceless attempts" to express an inner architecture. Because Lawrence was "patient" and listened to the murmurings of his dreams, and allowed them "to find their own way and hour of resurrection," he experienced them as fully as his nature and talents allowed. For Lawrence dreams took a long period of gestation: he waded "through a maze of timidities, retractions, blunders, awkwardnesses" (p. 10). But because of his "confidence in the wisdom of the body," Nin continued, he succeeded in extracting their living essence, their blood fibers.

Huxley, in *Point Counterpoint* and Gide in *The Immoralist* also attempted to discover their inner rumblings and to record them in their works. Unlike Lawrence, however, they were incapable of seizing minute vibrations, sense perceptions, and "physical visions" and give them the power and impulse necessary to set them on their own course. Huxley and Gide were cerebral. They stated their cases in categories of events and in arid delineations in which thoughts and sensations were analyzed to death. Their novels satisfied an intellectual curiosity because they used "that upper strata in the head," Nin wrote, therefore, "we were *hit in our heads*" and not in the viscera.

Lawrence went at the reversal of values not with indifference but with poetry, with religious fervor, and he hit lower than either Huxley or Gide. He hit the center, the vulnerable center of our bodies with his physical language, his physical vision. He hit us vitally. (p. 31)

Dreams have their own realities, pulsations, and spatial concepts, which must be experienced as flowing and active currents rather than as congealed images or static monuments in space. Dreams are like "vessels of steam from which live jets escape" that travel throughout the cosmos, condense, and relive their multidimensional course. Dreams are "inexhaustible reservoirs" for the creative individual who not only feels them but lives with them and experiences their moods and sensations in accordance with their level of consciousness.

For the ancient Egyptian, Hebrew, and Greek, the dream had mantic and healing powers, and it was so important that it was used as a part of initiation rituals. *Initiation* affords individuals entry into new spheres: a real inner journey. Plutarch described initiation ceremonies as a descent into "a marvelous light during which the neophyte passes into pure realms and prairies resound with voices and dances, with sacred words, and divine apparitions inspire religious respect."[7]

For Lawrence and Nin the dream was also a sacred ritual that caused entry into the realm of the mysterious and supernatural. The dream takes the external world and internalizes it, thus arousing the creative impulse. Balzac's dazzling imagination was forever inspired by his subliminal realm. Descartes's mathematical discoveries were first conceived after he had had three important dreams. F. A. Kekulé had tried for many years to express the molecular structure of trimethylbenzene graphically and succeeded only after seeing the image in his dreams. Dreams are a kind of fourth dimension where the space/time continuum comes into existence. Perceived by the artist, the dream is then molded by him in his own subjective and individual manner.

Symbols

"The symbol," wrote C. G. Jung, "is the best possible expression of what is still unknown."[8] It allows a universe of indeterminate dimension, incandescent feelings, and mobile essences to be glimpsed. The symbol may be expressed as a metaphor, an image, a feeling, harmony, rhythm, and in many other ways. It is alive and maintains its dynamism as long as it holds meaning for the individual projecting upon it, or as long as it is capable of arousing impulses and instincts. For medieval man, religious objects became hierophanies: sacred forces that triggered powerful reactions. In modern times few painters are inspired by this symbology: others, the machine, the body, and nature have emerged and replaced them.

Energy is interwoven into the substance of the living symbol. As such, it is transformed into a "magnetic field." It is comparable, to a certain extent, to a living volcano: if the energy enclosed in the symbol remains repressed in the artist's unconscious, it may explode, influencing his creative vision, even deforming it as in Picasso's case during his Blue Period, or as in Henry Moore's case with his rounded and circular forms. The energy stored in the living symbol sets up a dialectical relationship between conscious and unconscious factors; as such, the symbol is said to act as "psychic transformer" rendering manifest that which lies drowsily in the depths of man. As long as the symbol does not become overly rational, that is, impoverished by the light of reason, its dynamism will not wither. It will continue to stir, activate, and inspire the artist. But once its mystery has been revealed by prolonged explications and by sterile analytical studies, its affective nature is drained.

For Lawrence and Nin, the symbol became a means of perpetuating their search for self-discovery and increased consciousness. It conveyed feelings of immediacy; it fired the flux of excitement—the ecstasy of actuality. Nin wrote of Lawrence:

He takes the old symbol of the swan and interprets it in the light of his own vision: the swan would be the vital flame, the pure animal spirit. (p. 81)

The symbol was an active instrument that enabled Lawrence to penetrate substance and to experience the "thick, fierce darkness of the senses," the tingling feelings of abstractions. "The personages in his books are symbolical," Nin wrote, and because of such an approach, they are "preoccupied with subconscious acts, moods, and reactions." Symbols encouraged Lawrence to chart new ways. "His characters act by deeper and more chaotic motives than those in ordinary novels: they are experiments—subjected to all the shiftings of experimental living" (p. 20).

Symbols express not only a powerful sexual "craving", but also "the creator's craving for a climax far bigger than the climaxes life has to offer." It is a kind of "creative voraciousness which is, as a general instinct, unsatisfiable" (p. 21). This was certainly so in Lawrence's case, a man forever in pursuit of his creative urge. Whenever a symbol had become nonfunctioning or had grown arid, Lawrence moved to another land, to a different scene (England, Germany, Australia, the United States, Italy, France), always in search of environments and their symbols, areas that would enable him to experience that "disordering of the senses," that uprooting of what was solidly implanted—the experience mystics label "correspondences."

The theory of correspondences has affinities with the mystic beliefs of Heraclitus, Hermes Trismegistus, and the neo-Platonists. They believed that all in the universe is linked and related via intricate sets of correspondences that originate in God (or in a transpersonal immutable force) and appear to man as manifestations of Him. Because of such oneness, man is connected to everything: he is the microcosm within the macrocosm—man in God. Primordial oneness becomes differentiated in the manifest world in the form of trees, flowers, metals, rocks; each takes on its individual shape, its specific qualities. It is the artist's task to return to primordial oneness—to that invisible, impalpable, indiscernible region—the tremulous world of the uncreated. It is within the macrocosm (in the poet's case, his limited inner world) that he knows the incandescence and the tincture of adventure and discovers the symbols he feels may best convey these new experiences. In the poem "Correspondence," Baudelaire talked of trees that were alive and spoke to him in their own mysterious language—"a forest of symbols" that frightened him because these forms were concretizations of the ineffable. Nin wrote of Lawrence's *Mornings in Mexico*: "Sense of color, rhythm and form are keen and so is the understanding of their symbolic significance. There is also an almost occult mesmerism in his rhythmic repetitions" (p. 74). The symbol in its "infinite nuances" and in its "fullness and expansiveness" enabled Lawrence to experience renewal.

Nin warned, however, that Lawrence's books should not be understood "as great cosmic allegories" (p. 111). Abstractions, whether on the divine or human level, did not involve him. What he sought was "what he felt and experienced in himself," which he then molded into his characters. Because his personal experience was so profound, he succeeded in reaching that level common to all men—the transpersonal force.

His depth of perception allowed Lawrence to understand things that other writers could only touch upon. For Nin, the question of the female psyche was of importance and her admiration for Lawrence in this domain was great. He understood the problem of women who had been brought up to efface their "real self in order to satisfy man-made images" (p. 55). A woman's life had to follow a certain pattern from the day she was born; she had to act according to man's vision of her. Dante had his Beatrice, Dickens his child-wife; the young man had his "little-boy-baby-face girl." If a man sought such a girl, Lawrence stated, "What could she possibly give him but the dribblings of an idiot?" (p. 56). In *Give Her a Pattern*, Lawrence suggested that the unconscious has its own logic, geological folds, and ways of seeing and feeling that the conscious mind cannot understand. As Nin wrote, the woman likewise has her own logic and feelings.

A woman may spend years living up to a masculine pattern. But in the end the strange and terrible logic of emotion will work out the smashing of the pattern, if it has not been emotionally satisfactory. (p. 55)

Both Lawrence and Nin believed that only when a woman *knows herself authentically* can she become independent and mold her artistic creation, or her life, from her own fibers, essences, and earthiness. Independence is not only crucial for the woman as an artist but also for the woman in love. Nin declared:

When a man and woman truly come together, when there is a marriage, an unconscious vital connection is established between them like a blood-circuit. A man may forget a woman entirely with his head, and fling himself with energy and fervor into whatever job he is tackling, and all is well, all is good, *if he does not break* that inner vital connection which is the mystery of marriage. (p. 61)

To develop an individual's potential and allow independence of spirit to emerge is to encourage development and evolution as a human being and as a creative force:

Human love, human trust, are always perilous, because they break down. The greater the love, the greater the trust, and the greater the peril, the greater the disaster. Because to place absolute trust on another human being is in itself a disaster, both ways, since each human being is a ship that must sail its course, even if it go in company with another ship. (p. 65)

Because of Lawrence's understanding of the female ideology, feelings, and temperament as well as of the male's, Nin called his writing androgynous. His intuitive powers and his reasoned way of articulating sensations allowed him to present his readers with a "double point of view."

In all the descriptions of conflict the man and the woman's response is equally stated. He [Lawrence] is absolutely conscious of the twofold currents, in even measures. (p. 69)

Nin's "unprofessional study" of Lawrence's works succeeded in liberating her "not from idealism but from dead ideals" (p. 36). Her probings into Lawrence's characters, situations, and credos were really a sounding out of self through projection. It offered her literary as well as psychological therapy. Her immersion into Lawrence's world was an initiation into the mysterious domain of the artist and the devices needed to pursue the creative journey. It allowed her to experience those "dark gods" that live inchoate in all beings, including herself. Nin now realized that they had to be brought to light, understood, and assimilated in the work of art she was about to create—the prose poem *House of Incest*.

3

House of Incest

As mentioned in the previous chapters, Nin had always believed that the dream was a source of nourishment for the creative instinct. It became the *sine qua non* of her work. Dreams Nin had had for more than a year are presented in *House of Incest* in the form of two symbolic and parallel narratives. The first concerns lesbian love; the second, an incestuous relationship. Both disclose a world with which Nin felt at ease and to which she related; both are delineated in biomorphic images that fluctuate in shape, texture, form, and intensity; both lead to a domain that has its own logic, patterns, and language.

To consider the unconscious as a source of inspiration was implicit in the Surrealist credo, for the poet, the painter, and the musician. Surrealism used the techniques of automatic writing, free association, and reverie. Although Nin was never officially a member of this group, she wrote that "Surrealism was part of the air we breathed."[1] She empathized with the excitement and yearnings of these fervent and talented young people and followed their battles, loves, and obsessions. The Surrealists' longing for the marvelous and the fantastic and their belief in the unconscious as a storehouse of riches are also part of Nin's literary venture in *House of Incest*.

Surrealism

The publication of *The Surrealist Manifesto* in 1924 by André Breton marked the official founding of this group.

Breton defined Surrealism as a liberating and constructive force, one that would free man from the grasping tentacles of an overly constricting, moralistic bourgeois society as well as from literary and artistic conventions. Surrealism brought forth another world to be scrutinized, one not limited by rational vision but unconscious and infinite. The Surrealists sought to expand humanity's conception of reality, to make it reflect the totality of the universe. To accomplish this goal the creative individual had to commit himself to his unconscious world; he had to allow the inner realm to speak unhampered by any preconceived thoughts and judgments concerning time, space, and motion. The Surrealists rejected everything that was fixed or regulated. They wanted to become "the deaf receptacles of so many echoes, modest RECORDING INSTRUMENTS of another world." The unconscious was as real for them as the material world for most people. Breton wrote: "Surrealism is based on the belief in the superior reality of certain forms of association heretofore neglected, on the omnipotence of dreams, on the undirected play of thought."[2] Poets such as Louis Aragon, Paul Eluard, and Robert Desnos and painters such as Max Ernst, Joan Miró, and André Masson explored the unconscious. Breton further declared: "I believe in the future resolution of the states of dreams and reality, in appearance so contradictory, in a sort of absolute reality, or *surréalité*, if I may call it that."[3]

Breton's fascination with the unconscious dated perhaps from his service during World War I in neuropsychiatric centers and from his studies of Freudian theories. Psychiatric circles in France and Germany were burgeoning with new theories and fresh approaches to that ever mysterious and elusive inner world. Let us recall that Freud had gone to Paris in 1896, attracted by Dr. Jean Martin Charcot's experiments at the Salpêtrière in telepathic phenomena, hypnosis, and diverse antirational manifestations of psychic life. Charcot was the great specialist in hysteria and aphasia.

He believed that paralysis of the limbs was related to emotional problems and used hypnosis as a curative agent.
Freud also went to Nancy where Liébault and Bernheim
practiced posthypnotic suggestion in curing not only hysteria
but also other, milder psychoneurotic disorders. Pierre Marie
Félix Janet, who believed that hysteria was caused by a
fundamental weakness in the nervous system, also practiced
hypnosis to study the traumatic experiences, recalled in these
sessions, that had set off the neurotic symptoms within his
patients. In his *Psychopathia Sexualis* (1866), Richard von
Krafft-Ebing went into detail on the sexual aberrations indulged in by the mentally unbalanced.[4]

Until the end of the nineteenth century, psychiatrists
had turned their attention only to exceptional cases: perverts
and psychopaths, or the so-called degenerate genius. In this
way the rest of society could look upon themselves as blame-
less, clean, and righteous in their comportment. Victorian
ways had impressed upon people that anything that strayed
from the norm should be repressed because it was "unholy,"
an emanation from hell and un-Christian. By the early
twentieth century, however, the situation had changed. Psychiatrists became interested in the unexceptional neurotic
patient. Joseph Dejerine, professor of psychiatry at the
Salpêtrière, understood early in his practice that he could
not appeal to a patient on rational grounds, and declared:
"From my point of view psychotherapy depends wholly and
exclusively upon the beneficial influence of one person on
another,"[5] that is, patient and psychiatrist had to work together. In 1895 Josef Breuer and Freud published *Studies on
Hysteria*, and that year Freud developed the method of free
association. During the psychoanalytic session he would ask
his patients to give up conscious control of ideas, notions,
and credoes; they were to say anything that came to mind.
Unconscious material seeks expression, Freud maintained.
Uncontrolled thought allows the psychiatrist to view the tensions and conflicts through another dimension and to study

them through "the art of interpretation," which he set forth in his opus *Interpretation of Dreams* (1900).[6]

The Surrealists likewise used various techniques in poetry, music, and art in an endeavor to disrupt conscious orientation and thus allow the inner rumblings to emerge intact in full view of consciousness. Laughter, for example, was considered the easiest and most incisive way of destroying logical outlooks. Humor disrupts. It is an instrument of rebellion. It levels habitual rapports between two or more objects. In his essay "On Laughter," Bergson pointed out that "Humor alone injects something new, grotesque, hallucinatory into its surroundings." Ernst had a proclivity for humor. In "La Femme 100 Tête," he used objects from other mediums and associated them in disconcerting ways, thereby injecting an element of surprise and chance into his work. Paul Klee's humorous doodlings went beyond rational boundaries in expressing the workings of his unconscious.

Madness was also incorporated in the Surrealist credo. Insanity crushed the chains that bound man to the rational sphere. It expanded his possibilities. Incoherencies in speech and thought patterns offered a whole new world for the poet and for the artist. According to Freud, the insane know more about their world than the rational person does. If given the chance, the ravings of a madman may reveal untold secrets, and it is up to the psychiatrist to explain these in rational terms. Artaud described his eclipses of consciousness in harrowing schizophrenic interludes in his *Correspondence with Jacques Rivière*. Oedipus, Narcissus, and Electra complexes were popular subjects for the literary man, as were psychopathic illnesses such as paranoia and schizophrenia.

Nin considered the unconscious not only as a source of creativity, but also as a force to be used in healing people of their emotional and psychological ailments. She began to peer into its folds and started to discover her own primitive nature, her yearnings and torments. To face her inner world, however, required courage. To articulate and then record her dreams was torture for her. Yet, each time visions emerged from her unconscious, she encouraged them to evolve and burgeon. It was like giving birth to a child, she wrote. And the postpartum separation that followed, with its ensuing loneliness and agitation, was harrowing. Her nights seemed filled with clusters of eidetic images: biomorphic shapes, meandering lines, hybrid fantasies, colored intonations, metamorphoses of all types, including crystals, metals, fire, and water. All of these configurations are imbricated in *House of Incest*. The starting point of her visions is nearly always suggested by some material object—a room, floor, window, or necklace—or by sensations, such as the sun's warm rays or the moon's coldness. As the Surrealist poets Eluard, Desnos, Aragon, and Breton described their universe of beauty and ugliness, mystery and marvel, so Nin in youthful exaltation as well as in charged and incandescent visions conveyed her feelings and the inroads they made upon her in her journeys inward. For Nin, as for the Surrealists, language was not a deadened instrument but the recipient, the echo, the receptacle of an imponderable world.

Surrealism, with its emphasis on the subliminal realm as a creative and curative factor, did not satisfy Nin. Suffering from a tormenting lack of self-confidence and still feeling the pain and void that came with her father's desertion of the family, her condition had reached obsessive proportions. She wanted to gain self-knowledge and used art and language as the means to restore psychic balance in her life. She knew, however, from the outset of her therapeutic sessions, that the probing experience would be difficult and that it would entail sacrifice on her part. But life, she reasoned, is a process of transformation and entails perpetual immolation—the death of one state and the creation of another. Sacrifice looked upon in this manner becomes a sacred ritual, as the root of the word indicates. It must be faced with composure, courage, and consciousness.

The Therapeutic Process

The therapeutic process for Nin was an initiation ritual into an unknown realm, a reconstruction of one's knowledge of life. To gain such information requires probing, a sounding out of the forces within. Both René Allendy, with whom Nin underwent analysis first, and then Otto Rank, who succeeded him, aided her in different ways to decipher the meaning of the strange clusters of forms that emerged from her unconscious. Both men encouraged her to record her dreams and their minutest vibrations, the feelings they conveyed, and the impact they made. *House of Incest* was the outcome in large measure of Nin the patient and the psychotherapeutic sessions working in conjunction with Nin the artist.

René Allendy (1889–1942) was well-known in medical circles as the doctor who had introduced psychoanalysis into criminal court cases; and he was also known as the founder of the Société Française de Psychanalyse.[7] He was a mystic of sorts and was fascinated with alchemy, numerology, and astrology, as his thesis *Alchemical Theories in the History of Medicine* (1912) indicated. Allendy was convinced that destiny follows the dictates of one's unconscious will; that one's actions are often repeated because there are profound desires within a human being that urge a reenactment of the same or similar events and situations. An individual projects this inner force onto his environment and considers external reality rather than himself to be responsible for things if they do not turn out as he wishes. If one is determined enough, Allendy believed, a person can control fate to a large extent. But in order to do so, one has to understand inner motivations. To succeed in bringing unconscious forces to the light of consciousness requires an almost Buddhistlike discipline.

Allendy spoke from experience. He had been gassed in 1915 and then developed tuberculosis. The medical men stated that he had no chance for survival. Allendy, however, decided differently. He did not accept the destiny predicted. Not only did he succeed in arresting his tuberculosis; he also developed his capacity for work after his recuperation to formidable proportions. He had a private practice, attended hospitals, wrote many books, and enjoyed friendships. Psychoanalysis, he suggested, could bring about the enlightenment necessary to permit an individual to escape from his misfortune—his *karma*.[8]

Nin benefited greatly from Allendy's positive outlook, his intuitive nature, his understanding of her insecurity and the void her father's insensitivity had created. In her *Diary*, Nin wrote that Allendy's "patriarchic air" and bearded face made him resemble a "magician." And he did play the role of spiritual father and shaman in her life at this time. Early in their sessions, Allendy had expressed an interest in the plight of women in general and hers in particular. He confessed that psychiatrists knew little about the functioning of women's inner world.

Women have contributed nothing to psychoanalysis. Women's reactions are still an enigma, and psychoanalysis will remain imperfect as long as we have only men's knowledge on which to base our assumptions. We assume that a woman reacts like a man, but we do not know.

Nin was evolving as woman and artist. She wanted to continue her sessions but found it problematic to raise the money to maintain treatment. Allendy suggested she could do research work for him. Because *Alchemy and Medicine* (1912), *Dream and Psychoanalysis* (1926), and *Orientation of Medical Ideas* (1932) were some of his many volumes that fascinated her, Nin agreed, and he sent her to libraries to gather information on magic, rituals, and other esoterica as well as medical topics about which he was writing articles and books. In this manner her sessions were paid and she broadened her own knowledge.

Allendy's approach to his patients was Freudian and

scientific. His relentless probing and reductive analyses of dreams, reveries, and free association were cut and dry. He did not, Nin wrote, "understand the artist"; he saw "with his eyes."[10] His world was devoid of poetry, of the marvelous, of exaltation for life, of that youthful resiliency inbred in the creative person's vital organs. Allendy wanted his patients to adapt to life, to the mundane world—to be normal. Nin knew that she could never resemble the masses, nor did she want to. Her views on life were hers, and they were different from those expressed by the status quo. Her artistic temperament reacted according to its own makeup and logic. What she sought to accomplish was to discover its patterns, reflexes, and language.

Nin then consulted Dr. Otto Rank, whose work *Art and the Artist* (1932) had impressed her. His attitude was different from Allendy's. He was aware of the fact that his patients, particularly creative individuals, could not and should not even try to fit into a mold. Rank told Nin outright:

I place the emphasis on adaptation to an individual world. I want to increase your power of creation in order to sustain and balance the power of emotion which you have. The flow of life and the flow of writing must be simultaneous so that they can nourish each other. It is the revelation of creative activity which becomes a channel of redemption for the neurotic obsessions. Life alone cannot satisfy the imagination.[11]

Rank (1884–1939) was born in Vienna and had been one of Freud's closest disciples and protégés. He separated from his master after the publication of *The Trauma of Birth* (1924) and moved to Paris in 1926. In *The Trauma of Birth*, Rank suggested that the newborn's physiological responses (cardiac, respiratory) due to sensory stimulation were enormous and were the cause of future anxiety. A normal and healthy child is able to discharge his "primal anxiety" once he has separated from his mother; the neurotic, on the other hand, longs to return to the womb. Birth, whether physical or artistic, implies a severing, a kind of fall from a Garden of Eden, a type of death.[12]

Rank believed that Freud's emphasis on the sexual drive had turned man into a strictly biological creature, thus limiting his spiritual nature—the soul in him. That Freud put women in an inferior position with his patriarchal notions also displeased Rank. He claimed Freud suffered from an Oedipus complex and saw the world through his own subjective approach. And with Freud's suggestion that art was a manifestation of sublimated sexual instincts, Rank disagreed sharply. Rank held that because man felt a deep need to believe in the concept of immortality and could not accept death as an end to life, he sought to perpetuate his existence in the work of art. Embedded in the creation is the *soul*, that force within each human being that lives on eternally. If the creative drive as expressed in the *artist type* were merely a sublimated sexual impulse, Rank questioned, then what "diverted" it from its strictly biological function? What helped it to strive for expression in form? What directed it to become concretized in the poem, the painting, the piece of music?[13]

Rank distinguished between the artist type, whose psychic energy could be channeled into positive and creative outlets, and the *artiste-manqué*, the neurotic personality in whom energy has "gone wrong."[14] He further declared that human beings cannot be understood either empirically or metaphysically; extremes detract from the purely human aspect, from the mystery that is man. Rank marked the development of human consciousness in three stages: Apollonian: "know thyself"; Dionysian: "be thyself"; Kantian: "determine thyself from thyself."

The Apollonian stage is essentially Socratic in outlook. The mind, morality, and thinking processes must be developed in order to adapt to a "universal ideal" and to improve oneself accordingly. The Dionysian stage allows for an uninhibited expression of instinctual drives and leads to destruction or orgiastic ecstasy. "The true self, if it is unchained in Dionysian fashion, is not only anti-social but also unethical, and therefore the human being goes to pieces on it." In the case of the neurotic, the Dionysian phase is crucial: he seeks to be himself, that is, to allow his neurosis to strengthen and dominate his world. The Kantian view is an expression of "true self-knowledge and simultaneously an actual self-creation." It is the highest form of value; the paradigm of an individual creating himself, of molding himself according to his authentic nature.[15]

In *Art and Artist*, Rank suggested that the true artistic endeavor leads to the development of personality and is an expression of something personal as well as a remolding of the prevailing *Zeitgeist*. Thus it fuses the individual and the collective creation in an innovative form. It also links one's need for immortality with an "instinctive will to art." Rank further stated:

For the creative impulse in the artist, springing from the tendency to immortalize himself, is so powerful that he is always seeking to protect himself against the transient experience, which eats up his ego.

. . . In creation the artist tries to immortalize his mortal life. He desires to transform death into life, as it were, though actually he transforms life into death. For not only does the created work not go on living; it is in a sense, dead, both as regards the material, which renders it almost inorganic, and also spiritually and psychologically in that it no longer has any significance for its creator, once he has produced it. He therefore again takes refuge in life, and again forms experiences, which for their part represent only mortality—and it is precisely because they are mortal that he wishes to immortalize them in his work.[6]

Nin was impressed with Rank's knowledge and interest in the artist's personality. He, as Nin, had kept a diary, which he called *Daybooks* (1903–05), and therefore could understand from his own experience the importance such work holds for an individual who feels the weight of loneliness, rejection, and insecurity. Rank also considered himself an artist, "even if I never succeed in bringing forth a single work of art," as he wrote in his *Daybooks*. He was endowed with the temperament of the creative individual and needed an outlet to express his feelings and ideas. In the course of his work he discovered analogies between the poetic creation and the dream: both dreamer and writer convey feelings and images that would otherwise have been repressed in the workaday world. Important, too, was the fact that Rank was a fervent admirer of D. H. Lawrence. In fact, he considered that *The Fantasy of the Unconscious* had made Lawrence "the greatest psychological philosopher since Nietzsche because he was more human."[17] Rank also knew and admired Nin's close friend Henry Miller. He was convinced that Miller as a person transcended Miller the writer: only part of Miller's creative talents were revealed in his novels.[18]

Nin felt comfortable with Rank. She knew that he did not consider her obsessions and anxieties as illnesses, but rather "as in nature, a misbegotten object which might have equal beauty and fascination as the relative of more legitimate and noble birth. Neurosis was Spanish moss on a tree." It was of prime importance to Nin that Rank tried "to adapt each person to his own kind of universe" and that he believed "the creative instinct" must be encouraged and treated with love and understanding. Moreover, Rank's attitude toward women was virtually unique at this period. Whereas Allendy, although confessing his ignorance about the woman's inner world, still considered woman intellectually and psychologically inferior to man, Rank believed that little was known about the inner woman, since philosophers, psychologists, historians, and biographers were for the most part men. Only by probing into the unconscious could they gain access to the woman's mysterious world.[19]

Rank attempted to understand the individual and help him "reenact the process of creation," thereby remedying a malfunctioning psyche. Unlike Allendy, Rank looked for the solution within the individual. Each individual must explore his inner world and experience his neuroses fully to understand them so that needless suffering may be transformed into positive creative activity. There were no recriminations and no negative attitudes for Rank. Life is a composite of opposites and must be experienced as such. The quest for healing therefore entails pain and joy as well as the excitement engendered by self-discovery.

For Nin writing in conjunction with the therapeutic process had become a liberating and constructive force. Feelings of exaltation accompanied her flight to freedom, which followed the therapeutic process and the creation of *House of Incest*. "Immediately I felt air and space, movement, vitality, joy of detecting, divining."[20]

The Work in Creation

House of Incest, or as Nin described it, altering Rimbaud's words, "A Woman's Season in Hell," is a *discipline*: the artist in the process of giving birth to a work, of constructing an edifice. To build a novel, a prose poem, a cathedral, or a sculpture requires the full cooperation of the unconscious world—its dreams and images—as well as the application of the rational function. The material emerging from the subliminal world helter-skelter has to be sifted, evaluated, molded, and incorporated into the poet's visions, thus making for cohesion and wholeness.

Unlike Octave Mirbeau's *The Garden of Tortures* (1898), which had inspired Nin to write *House of Incest* but which depicted only physical pain, her work would broach emotional cruelties. "I felt obsessions and anxieties were just as cruel and painful, only no one had described them vividly, as vividly as physical tortures."[21] For Nin, the process of creation—whether it centered around the work of art, the emergence of an idea, or the development of a personality—was traumatic. She described this condition viscerally at the outset of *House of Incest*.[22]

The morning I got up to begin this book I coughed. Something was coming out of my throat: it was strangling me. I broke the

thread which held it and yanked it out. I went back to my bed
and said: I have just spat out my heart. (p. 1)

The word "creation" implies separation: the passage
from one state to another, one ontological level to the next.
For the writer, innovation implies a doing away with (at
least in part) past ideations, styles, and techniques. James
Joyce in *Ulysses* (1914–21), Virginia Woolf in *Mrs.
Dalloway* (1925), and Marcel Proust in *Remembrance of
Things Past* (1913) had all rejected the "well-made novel,"
so popular among their contemporaries, with its realistic
characters, its structured plots, its artifices used to create
suspense. Each in his own way brought a fresh approach to
the novel: the interior monologue, stream-of-consciousness
technique, use of involuntary memory to reintegrate past
experiences into present situations. Nin was not only impressed but also deeply moved by the poetic and symbolic
quality of the works of Joyce, Woolf, and Proust, the delicacy and sensitivity of their imagery, the penetrating insights, and the extraordinary evocation of moods. She
understood that the artistic process, if authentic, is an act of
courage. It is also an act of aggression that may bring down
the wrath of the critics or, worse still, may be ignored by
the reading public. Certainly Joyce, Woolf, and Proust had
had their share of critical disapproval and destructive and
negative reactions. Nin knew that her *House of Incest* would
likewise attract castigations from her contemporaries, her
family, and her friends.

Yet, artistic expression became a *modus vivendi* for
Nin and she realized, as Antonin Artaud had already discovered, that creativity was a cruel gift. To create, Artaud had
written in his essay "The Theatre and Cruelty," was a searing experience. Creation implies alteration. All transformatory processes entail motion and conflict, thus cruelty. When
God created the world, He did away with the original state
of unity. When He cast Adam and Eve from Paradise, he
further increased the division between man and Himself and

man and the cosmos. Man fell into the world of antagonism
—that is, life. Hence, when the artist gives birth to something new, he wrenches from himself the germ or the idea
embedded in his flesh, imbues it with breath and substance,
and nurtures it until it can care for itself. Once it becomes
an autonomous entity, it fends for itself in the harsh world
of consciousness. The birth of *House of Incest* was painful.
"I yearn to be delivered of this book," Nin wrote. "It is
devouring me."[23]

Lesbianism/Narcissism

The first tale in *House of Incest* concerns a lesbian
relationship. The narrator, after recounting her prenatal experiences and the freedom and ecstasy she felt in her fetal
condition, confesses her love for Sabina, a hard, domineering *femme fatale* type. Throughout the story Sabina is associated with cold, moonlike qualities. The narrator, on the
other hand, is warm and understanding and radiates sunlike
characteristics. We learn that the narrator and Sabina are in
fact two manifestations of the same person. The narrator is
pursuing her own image as reflected in her love object. She
yearns to blend within her and thus experience the original
state of prenatal unity. Such a quest leads to pain and to
feelings of nostalgia. As her passion for Sabina grows and
ecstasy follows the sexual experience, despair encroaches.
The narrator realizes now that she will never know wholeness. What she seeks in Sabina is union with herself.[24] As
the narrator slips in and out of moods, lovemaking, and
despair, her activity points to a fundamental rootlessness, an
inability to look within. The more passionate she becomes
and the more she yearns for union with Sabina, the more her
dependency on Sabina grows and the more dominated she
feels. She is forever seeing aspects of her own personality
projected on Sabina. Like Narcissus she is unconsciously in
love with herself.

In *House of Incest* the poetic image of two aspects of woman was pursued and became the two faces, the night and day faces, of woman, one all instinct, impulse, desire, impetus without control, the other who had sought control by awareness. The only danger, of course, is that one strong personality can submerge the other; one can feel the loss of himself in the other (as frequently can happen in love), but there is no life without danger, and the *other* danger, the danger of alienation (and through alienation, non love, or hatred, or destructiveness, dehumanization), I consider far greater.[25]

The narrator's personality fades into oblivion in one sequence; then an exchange of personalities occurs. "DOES ANYONE KNOW WHO I AM?" (p. 26) the narrator cries out in a frantic effort to orient herself, discover a meaning to her life, and find her ego. So dazed is she that she cannot even recognize any part of herself. Like a shattered mirror, she sees her splintered self: the rays, the reverberations are flying off into space. "Even my voice came from other worlds. I was embalmed in my own secret vertigoes" (p. 26). There is no limit to her torment. Linear time does not exist in her unconscious world; it cannot ground her. Nor does her shattered ego allow her to relate to the outside world or to differentiate inner and outer realms. She is wracked with fear—captivated, subdued, imprisoned by her sensations. She remains passive before Sabina's domineering ways. She loses herself in her double. "I AM THE OTHER FACE OF YOU" (p. 28), she tells Sabina as she moves about blindly, her faceless countenance bouncing back and forth in a rhythmic interplay between illusion and reality.

Hopelessness—the narrator knows she can never unite with her beloved Sabina and withdraws into her isolated realm. The agony of separation is evinced as the narrator experiences sensations of disintegration: the void within, the silent agony of solitude. "I die in a small scissor-arched room, dispossessed of my love and my belongings" (p. 32). For the mystic, the inner road leads to riches and infinity. As the narrator spans her disparate inner cosmos, its color levels and cuttings, "a dissolution of the soul and body" come to pass. She is overcome with a sense of emptiness and aridity. Consciousness is eclipsed. "Reality was drowned and fantasies choked each hour of the day" (p. 84). A prisoner of her world at the conclusion of the first part of Nin's prose poem, escape becomes impossible; torture, confusion, and anguish advance.

Homosexual love is an expression, Nin believed, of arrested psychological development. In some cases it may arise as a result of a poor relationship with one or both parents in childhood and lead to an inability to relate to one of the sexes. During adolescent years a girl might therefore find it easier to form close emotional ties with a member of her own sex simply because she had experienced a faulty relationship with her father. Homosexuality at this stage of development may be covert or sometimes overt. As maturity makes its inroads, however, heterosexual relationships usually displace the earlier homosexual loves.[26]

In the lesbian love between the narrator and Sabina, we are dealing with a woman who has reached an impasse in her psychological development. She suffers from an alienated ego. She is incapable of loving anyone because she herself feels unloved. To fall in love with an aspect of oneself (as reflected in another) indicates a longing to unite with that facet of oneself simply because it is alienated. Because it feels its solitude, it tantalizes, attracts, and also angers and dominates. The narrator needs and wants what she does not have. Because she feels unloved and frustrated, she yearns to possess Sabina, who knows that she is sought after and so hardens to the situation. To feel unloved leads to a blockage of libido, or psychic energy. Rather than exteriorize itself, this energy is driven inward. Rather than discovering new riches in the subliminal realm, it spreads decay.[27]

In Ovid's *Metamorphoses*, Narcissus falls in love with his reflection in a pool of water and dies of despair because he cannot possess the object of his passion. Narcissus is an adolescent who still lives in a state of *participation mystique* —that is, in self-containment that exists prior to the birth of consciousness. His ego is in a state of primary identity with self. As his name indicates, Narcissus is tired and passive.[28] Unlike the ancient hero (or heroine) who seeks new experiences through quests and journeys far from home—in the exogamous experience—Narcissus is content to remain at home. Battles and struggles (aspects of the hero's personality and lot) indicate, psychologically, a powerful and aggressive nature necessary to build and strengthen an individual's ego. Narcissus, however, never broaches the outside world. He is self-contained, involved only with himself. His image, or umbra, is reflected before him and he is absorbed in its contemplation. His mother, Liriope, had asked the blind seer Tiresias when her son was born whether he would live to a ripe old age. "Yes," answered Tiresias, "if he never knows himself." But Narcissus did "know" himself in the pool of water before him, and because of the image with which he fell in love, he realized he could never experience independence and wholeness and so died from the agony of this realization.

Lesbian love as experienced by the narrator and Sabina is also narcissistic. Rather than channeling the libido outward, it is interiorized, reflected on itself. Rather than discovering the wealth of riches in the unconscious, and from these nutrients developing and evolving, energy is "deflected into an endopsychic activity"[29] and attaches itself to still-born aspects of itself, thus limiting its growth and becoming pathological.[30] The "reflection instinct" is constantly turning back upon itself, dragging everything that impedes its inward journey with it, and therefore no progression in the relationship between the narrator and Sabina can occur. Activity exists, but it is perpetually leading to an impasse. Because the narrator loves Sabina, a masculine type woman, it might be said that she identifies her with rationality and consciousness incorporating both within herself. The narrator says, "I see two women in me freakishly bound together. I see them tearing away from each other. I can hear the tearing, the anger and love, passion and pity" (p. 30).

The narrator knows that she is caught between the image and its reflection as in a hall of mirrors. Like Narcissus, she is without identity, possessed and not autonomous. Rather than viewing the external world realistically and experiencing it objectively, her libido is dammed up, forcing her back into her solipsistic realm, into stagnation and death. "To nourish illusion. To destroy reality" (p. 26). Love for an outside object is excluded under such circumstances. She can relate only to objects through fantasy images, which leads to further fragmentation, to increased split-offs, and more distortions. The narrator has sinned. She has offended Eros, the god of relatedness. Anchored in her own world, her unrealized soul knows only alienation.[31]

Incest/Narcissism

The second tale revolves around incest. Jeanne, lame in one leg—a symbol for her unbalanced psychological outlook and her inability to relate to the workaday world—is in love with her brother. Although she never expresses her passion overtly, her obsession with him manifests itself when she kisses his shadow and when she feels imprisoned in his presence. She confesses her guilty love to the narrator of the first tale, then leads her into "the house of incest" with its small windows and endless rooms. Jeanne loses her brother in this labyrinthine realm. After a frantic search, she finds him hidden in a secret room. The blinds are drawn; all is closed. A static and sterile quality reigns. Jeanne desires her brother. Aware now that her feelings will never be gratified, she withdraws into her own realm as the narrator had done in the first story.

The incestuous love Jeanne feels for her brother is as narcissistic as the passion the narrator had experienced for Sabina. The situations are parallel: the subjects are in love with their own unconscious characteristics projected onto a woman and onto a brother, respectively. The libido is blocked in both the lesbian and incestuous experiences, and is doomed in advance.

Considered unclean and unholy and punishable by death in many societies, incest may be understood, psychologically, as the force that impedes new blood, new ties, and new contacts from taking root. The incest as depicted in the Oedipus myth continued the pattern of endogamy considered dangerous for the well-being and future development of a group and therefore had to be stopped. Psychologically, in the Oedipal situation, energy was flowing back into the family cell and not outward. The incest taboo forced individuals to reach beyond what they had, to discover exciting worlds, practice extroversion, and enjoy new biological and family ties. It fostered aggressivity, expanded horizons, spurred efforts, and strengthened the ego.[32]

Lesbianism, "the union of like with like" in the form of homosexual relationships, wrote C. G. Jung, marks "the stage preceding the brother-sister incest."[33] Hence, it was perfectly fitting that Nin placed the lesbian narrative before the one dealing with incest. Jung further declared that the archetype of incest is a restatement of the notion that "the father is reborn in the son" and so becomes part of the death-rebirth pattern in nature.[34] "Christ is said to have created Mary and thus fathered her in order to bear him as her son."[35]

In Nin's tale the brother symbolizes "the first step beyond the father." Jeanne, then, is not projecting on her own sex (as the narrator did in the first story), but on a male: *the son of the father.* She has gone one step beyond the father image. Brother and sister are equals. They are of the same age and can play out their fantasy games symbolically. The brother, an animus projection to be sure, is a concretization of Jeanne's male (spiritual and intellectual) characteristics, which until this time had lain dormant within her unconscious. As the brother plays out the fantasies, he becomes a catalyst, paving the way for his sister's inner transformation at the conclusion of the tale.

Incestuous psychological relationships in modern society occur frequently when home life is unhappy or when an individual feels insecure and unloved. If the transitional stages (from daughter to father to brother to outside male) can be accomplished, fruitful external relationships can be experienced. If, however, a girl's animus (a boy's anima), is unable to be projected and the fantasies are therefore perpetually repressed, pathological situations may arise. The problem is then fixated at the infantile level, as in Edgar Allan Poe's *The Fall of the House of Usher*. But Jeanne's situtation in relation to her brother is more positive. She experiences the first two stages of the initiation process (from father to brother) because she is able to indulge in her fantasies with her brother. She plays out the erotic-sexual aspect of the relationship. "I LOVE MY BROTHER!" she cries out (p. 46). When she leads the narrator into her house of incest, she is aware of the fact that the rooms are "chained together by steps . . ." (p. 51), that nothing moves and that the atmosphere is static. Though there are windows, the protagonists are blind; though the "rhythmic heaving of the sea" floods the room, a motionless world exists within— sterility. "Everything had been made to stand still in the house of incest because they all had such a fear of movement and warmth, such a fear that all love and all life should flow out of reach and be lost" (p. 52). Darkness, deathlike stillness, decay. No growth is allowed in this closed infantile world, no development, no rapport with anyone, not even with her brother whom she loves—the father "once removed."[36] The atmosphere of sterility and decay is conveyed in the imagery inspired by the sculptures of Zadkine and Brancusi.

I came upon a forest of decapitated trees . . . faces cut in two by the sculptor's knife, showing two sides forever separate, eternally two-faced, and it was I who had to shift about to behold the entire woman. Truncated undecagon figures, eleven sides, eleven angles, in veined and vulnerable woods, fragments of bodies, bodies armless and headless. (p. 55)

Whereas the narrator, when she realizes that sexual union with Sabina has not brought fulfillment withdraws into her inner world, Jeanne, when she becomes aware of the full impact of the endogamous tendency within her, does not withdraw "into darkness" to live in solitude but to spiritualize and sublimate her passion in the work of art. She is not alone in the house of incest. She sees a paralytic who has sought to move about but is incapable of mustering the force to drive away inertia and thus remains in a condition of stasis. Such would become her fate, Jeanne realizes, were she to allow her passivity to take hold. The "modern Christ, who is crucified by his own nerves," inhabits another area of the house. Finally an armless dancer, who seeks to show others the way out of the maze but cannot, speaks out: "I was punished for clinging. I clung. I clutched all those I loved; I clutched at the lovely moments of life; my hands closed upon every full hour." Yet, it is through the motions she makes, the whirling and swerving dance movements, that the personal pain the dancer knows is transformed into the collective feeling that leads to the daylight beyond.

And she danced; she danced with the music and with the rhythm of earth's circles; she turned with the earth turning, like a disk, turning all faces to light and to darkness evenly, dancing towards daylight. (p. 72)

The incest taboo is so deeply ingrained in Jeanne that it acts as a catalyst, leading her to eventual growth, evolution, and cultural progress. Once she has lived through the incestuous fantasies and they have been objectified in her brother, the personal experience is transmuted into the transpersonal image that is then expressed in the work of art—the book.[37]

The dance, a symbol of the creative effort, displaces the static visions in the secret room of the house; rhythms now flow forward, without fear or guilt, as did primitive and animistic sequences. Jeanne has succeeded in going beyond the father and the brother. The work of art might also be looked upon as a projection: as such Jeanne is again living out her incestuous and narcissistic fantasies in the creatures she describes in her book. Yet, differences exist. The libido used to create a character in a written work is not drawn back into the subjective sphere; rather it is activated and flows out onto the object—the paper.

Unlike Narcissus, who drowned when caught up in his own reflection, Nin chose another dimension—the word—to express her visions, thus paving the way for a closer relationship with reality. That Nin's dancer was "dancing towards daylight" indicated the author had become aware of the projection: she understood the meaning of her fantasies and their implication. She had successfully passed the preliminary initiatory rite: from the amorphous sensation to the concrete fantasm in the book, from the inner to the outer world. Divested of the personal element, *House of Incest* had become an impersonal drama imbued with mythological status and thus gained eternal validity.

An Alchemical Drama

Nin had learned much from the research work she had done for Dr. Allendy, particularly in the realm of alchemy, and she became fascinated by the psychological as well as by the artistic approach to this science. *House of Incest* may be looked upon as an alchemical drama. As the alchemist performs his transmutations, so the protagonists in *House of Incest* intuit their way through the seven chapters of the prose poem: the seven hells or heavens of the creative process, the seven days of Creation.

The symbols used in *House of Incest* (room, cave, water, house), like those employed by the alchemist, are, in C. G. Jung's words, "psychic transformers." They make visible what lies drowsily in the protagonist's depths and is not yet impoverished by the light of reason. Symbols, sources of dynamism, render the motionless movement active, the arid fertile. They stir the energy inherent in the archetypal image and compel it to rise to the surface or to consciousness. Its component parts are absorbed in the flesh, vivified and revivified in a ceaseless flow, then buried again deep within the elements. Thus the symbols' forms alter and their substance, molded into new shapes, impose fresh visions on the world, but never submit to it.

Complex forces are at work in *House of Incest*. Liquids confront solids and ideas attack sensations like acids biting into metals in sensual and provocative cadences, molding, forging, and blending in a eurythmic interplay of words, images, and feelings. Three alchemical stages are played out in the book: *nigredo, albedo, rubedo. Nigredo*, the blackening process, is comparable to the alchemist's chaos, to the *massa confusa* of the primordial condition, before separation of the elements or any psychological evaluation of the situation comes to pass. The narrator and Sabina live in an undifferentiated realm, and so do Jeanne and her brother. The "dark night of the soul" inhabits their worlds; solitude, a kind of spiritual dismemberment, is taking place: "A dissolution of the soul within the body like the rupture of sweet-acid of the orgasm" (p. 34). Within the chthonic sphere of the grotto/room, the seed of creation or of transformation is implanted: lesbian love grows, incestuous passion inflates, barriers vanish. Facelessness invades the atmosphere. Penumbra reigns. The narrator yearns for herself in Sabina; Jeanne longs to unite with herself in the form of her brother.

For the alchemist, blackness symbolizes withdrawal into a land of death, an eclipse of consciousness, a cutting off of mundane existence. Imprisonment in cavernous depths awaits the protagonists as do the terrors connected with the transformatory process: guilt, anxiety, fright, degradation, stagnation, decay. Such a descent into Self as the protagonists experience in parallel situations forces them to contact the most archaic spheres of their unconscious, that "inner firmament" where diamonds cut through their coverings and stand visible in all of their resplendence.

Similar to the athanor, a receptaclelike uterus, in which the alchemist cooks his many elements, seeking to transmute them into what he calls the Philosophical Egg, or "Stone," Nin's *House of Incest* "has the shape of an egg" (p. 34). It is a composite of blendings, solderings, moldings of metals, minerals, and chemicals into word images, word configurations, word language. "Our faces are soldered together by soft hair, soldered together, showing two profiles of the same soul" (p. 28).

From the black phase, the protagonists pass onto the next step of their initiatory process: the *albedo*, or white sphere. It is here that the washing of the elements in question takes place—that baptism occurs. The purification of the metals and crystals embedded in the protagonists' visions happens: mercury, sulphur, and salt are made immaculate. "I was the white flame of your breath. . . . I borrowed your visibility and it was through you I made my imprint on the world. I praised my own flame in you" (p. 28). In the whiteness of this burgeoning world, in its "silver," or "moon," condition as the alchemist calls it, the narrator begins to understand the nature of her love for Sabina; her black terror, or inner flow, is superseded by "the white path" that "sprouted from the heart of the white house" (p. 34). Whiteness upon whiteness is born, not always comforting, not always gentle. "I remember the cold on Jupiter freezing ammonia and out of ammonia crystals came the angels. Bands of ammonia and methane encircling Uranus" (p. 40).

Earthly metals become linked to the metal with which each of the seven astral bodies is associated: the Sun is gold, the Moon is silver, Venus is copper, Mercury is mercury, Mars is iron, Jupiter is tin, and Saturn is lead. As a representative of cosmic energy (or libido), metal has emotional value; it also takes on specific character traits. The baser metals, such as lead, apply to the visceral domain. Gold

symbolizes the highest spiritual values and represents a quintessence of all metals, a transmutation from lower to higher
forms: from constriction in the sense world to liberation of
the poet's creative energy in undifferentiated spheres—thus
causing the birth of the creative work.

From formlessness to a "fissure in reality," the head
emerges. The head is born in whiteness, "pulled up by the
clouds and swinging in space" (p. 34). Venus was born
from the foam of a wave. Nin's creation solidifies. Steel,
mercury, silver, mirrors, and crystals are incised in multiple
outpourings, appearing and disappearing in swift and successive configurations. Valued for their color and texture, they
are polished now and radiate with prismatic sheen, grada-
tions of whiteness in water. Jeanne leads the narrator into
her house of incest: "Further a forest of white plaster eggs.
Large white eggs on silver disks, an elegy to birth, each egg
a promise, each half-shaped nascence of man or woman or
animal not yet precise" (p. 56).

Water is the supreme baptism of the creative artist. And
water permeates and insinuates itself everywhere in the
House of Incest. It washes down and melts the minerals and
metals until all is fluid and pristine; it causes growth and
greenness. According to Thales, the principle of all things
resides in water. It stands for a world *in potentia*; for
virtuality, change, and perpetual motion. Like fire, water is a
transitional element, a mediator between life and death—the
poet and the creation. A watery surface can take on a
mirrorlike sheen as do polished marble and metal. A lake,
for example, can reflect celestial bodies, thereby unifying
heaven and earth. Larger expanses of water have hypnotic
qualities about them; their perpetual motion mesmerizes.
When water is aroused, it grows into cataclysmic force, as in
floods. Once it subsides, as it does in *House of Incest*, new
permutations and fresh visions come into being. Water
changes the destiny of the creative artist. It has also a sacred
quality, such as holy water, and becomes capable of mira-
cles. Baptism absolves from original sin. Initiation through

water permits access to cosmic realism for the mystic. Water is linked to the unconscious and, accordingly, to the female principle. Within this undifferentiated body inhabited by the uncreated live innumerable riches inchoate. Under proper stimulus, water gives birth to creativity.

My first vision of earth was water veiled. I am of the race of men and women who see all things through this curtain of the sea, and my eyes are the color of water. . . .

I remember my first birth in water. All around me a sulphurous transparency and my bones move as if made of rubber. I sway and float, stand on boneless toes listening for distant sounds, sounds beyond the reach of human ears, see things beyond the reach of human eyes. (p. 15)

Here Plato's myth of reincarnation, Plotinus's "Original Soul," and Emerson's "Oversoul" are alluded to. Nostalgia for the primordial condition is experienced. But as water creates, so it destroys when consciousness is overpowered by unconscious forces and leads to the dissolution of the ego.

Water permits the narrator and Jeanne to immerse themselves into the *fons et origo*—that is, to return to a preformal stage, a new beginning, and the possibility of altering the word/image. Mesmerized by the rhythmic patterns of the water, the protagonists savor its cleasing character and experience its undulations as an aid to meditation. They are lulled into an almost trancelike state, faceless, and without identity. Then they flash and thrash around. To inhabit the undifferentiated sphere for any length of time leads to a reintegration with preexistence. As Gaston Bachelard noted: "The person vowed to water is a person in vertigo. He dies at every instance."[38]

In *House of Incest* the narrator emerges from her depths, her "arched room," from her "empty house."

I hear the unfurling of water, of skies and curtains. I hear the shiver of leaves, the breathing of the air, the wailing of the unborn, the pressure of the wind.

I hear the movements of the stars and planets, the slight rust creak when they shift their position. The silken passage of radiations, the breath of circles turning. (p. 38)

The narrator has imbibed the waters of Mnemosyne, enabling her to recall anterior existences (thus knowing the meaning of life and death), and drunk from the River Lethe, which offers her forgetfulness and oblivion. She has brought her bounty from her depths, the riches, "mysteries," and "monsters" that are hers in nuanced hallucinations and in accelerated rhythmic patterns as well as in eloquent silences and frenzied forms. "Collision with reality blurs my vision and submerges me into dream. I feel the distance like a wound" (p. 38). And "rock crystal eyes," "a sea-diamond," and a "steel necklace" form.

Crystals come from and are transported by water. They are creators of light as well as barriers to vision. Like shining stars in a uniform landscape, so crystals are clues to riches hidden within blackness. An object of contemplation, crystals have a hypnotic effect upon the creative artist like water, depending upon the regularity, the motility, and the depth of the rays of light shining upon them. Crystals can become things of beauty—in the form of diamonds or shiny steel—and draw individuals into their embrace. By the same token they are cold bodies. The Greek word *crystal* is derived from "ice" or "frozen water." It was thought in ancient times that stones produced crystals only in extreme cold and in the high altitude of the Alps. In his *Natural History* (Book II), Pliny wrote that no art can equal the beauty of rock crystals with their icelike purity and their stonelike transparency. The alchemist Albertus Magnus believed that ice was so dry in the highest mountain tops that it congealed into crystals. In Job (28:17), crystals are compared to wisdom, although unequal to it; in Revelations (4:6), a terrifying vision is embedded in crystals.

In the last phase of the alchemical process—*rubedo*, or redness—the alchemist heats his elements, and under the intense fire, they turn red and all impurities are extracted from them. The conjunction of opposites comes into being and with it the creation of the "Philosopher's Stone." Fire, a most important principle in the transformatory process, penetrates hard bodies and transforms disparate metals and minerals into gold. The spectrum alters.

Fire is fluid. It gives warmth and light, electricity, movement, and energy. Fire is also passion. It is volatile and virtual; it illuminates and permits vegetation to grow. It destroys, calcinates, deforms, and blinds. In the *House of Incest*, flames with copper, gold, blood, crimson, rust, coral, pomegranate, and candlelight flood the scene. The "womb and seed and egg" are ready to be born. Passion is at its height: the narrator experiences ecstasy in Sabina's arms; Jeanne knows the heat of love at the very thought of her brother's body.

Gold and riches of vision become the supreme illumination. The word *gold* (*aor*, in Hebrew, meaning "light"; *aurum*, in Latin) is equated with intuition. The Kabbalists believed that within the earth there existed a godly light that had been lost after "the breaking of the vessels" and the dispersion of Adam Kadman, the primordial man. Within matter, then, there reside both light and heat. Embedded in this *prima materia*, the protagonists experience the infinite. From this vantage point, selections of crystallized essences are decanted slowly and luxuriantly throughout the work. They are polished, rubbed down with firm and loving strokes, until they sparkle and burn in gemlike formation.

The passion they feel allows the protagonists to reveal their inner riches and to come to terms with their guilt, fear, and traumas, which they do by weaving their anguishes in undulating dancelike patterns—like Shiva and his Cosmic Dance. The narrator and Jeanne observe the armless dancer at the finale of *House of Incest*. This impersonal figure intertwines time and space, like the Hindu divinity, who protected by a circle of flame controls the vital rhythms—the creative drive.

House of Incest has been constructed by the artist. It holds its mysterious powers in its giant heart. Libod Drusu, the Roman magician mentioned by Tacitus in his *Annals*, had incantatory power; the same may be said of the prose poem that allows contact to be made with past, present, and future in a simultaneous image of sensory visualizations. As architect of *House of Incest*, the creative artist evolved and originated unknown correspondences of patterns and organizations of space, form, color, and material in an interplay of abstract and concrete relationships. The word "architect" implies a fashioner of monuments, pyramids, cathedrals, and temples—buildings that inhabit cyclical time schemes and integrate cosmic patterns, thereby lending a sense of nostalgia and continuity to the unpredictable.

Nin wrote in *House of Incest*, "I describe what it is to be trapped in the dream, unable to relate to life, unable to reach 'daylight.' " It is in this nightmarish atmosphere that the alienated ego activates inner images; that color and texture convey feeling; that horror invades the identity-less creatures peopling the house, each attempting to devour the other, each succumbing to or weakened by the other—in reality, the narcissistic ego. Unloved and alienated, they finally make their way out of the labyrinth—into "daylight."

It was Henry Miller who aroused Nin's "fighting spirit" and her "strength," she said, who "forced" her to "write a bigger book." *House of Incest* took courage to write because Nin not only had to overcome her own sense of shame at her confession but her family's antagonistic attitude toward the book and, perhaps, society's as well. Nin might not have had the courage and inner strength necessary to overcome the ordeal of rejection and disapproval had she not had the therapeutic help and affection of Dr. Allendy and Dr. Rank.

When publishers began rejecting *House of Incest*, Henry Miller kept Nin's spirits buoyed up: "Get out the *House of Incest*, dust it up and send it round to someone else. Don't wait for a rainy day. Don't be discouraged. *This is war.*[39]

It would be war. There was no turning back now. No more imprisonment in the image and its reflection, nor in the abysmal darkened secret room of *House of Incest.* The artist in her *willed to create*; Nin *willed to succeed*!

4

~~~~~~

Antinovelettes:
Winter of Artifice
and *The Voice*

Winter of Artifice and *The Voice* do not adhere to the
conventional techniques of the short novel and its structured
characters and linear plots. As antinovelettes, they feature
clusters of pastiches with little or no story line and no progressive character delineations. Nin uses the literary devices
of repetitions, omissions, ellipses, dream sequences, and
stream-of-consciousness insertions that interrupt the free-
flowing atmosphere, jarring the reader into a new state of
awareness and plunging him into the penumbral void.
Juxtapositions of images occur and recur with differing
nuances, and like painful and joyous litanies that distort the
atmosphere, they heighten tension and pave the way for
what have been called nonverbal zones: wordless images
articulated via musical tonalities and associations.

Winter of Artifice[1] is the story of Djuna, who ido-
lizes her father. She has not seen him for twenty years
and, as the story opens, awaits his visit. Valescure in the
South of France is the idyllic setting for their meeting. In
her father's company she experiences a range of emotions:
from ecstasy, when she looks upon herself as her father's
"mystical bride," to depression, when she realizes that her
Prince Charming father is an illusion, a figment of her imagination. In reality her father is a superficial, luxury-loving,
and rigid man who lives for externals only. The love they
feel for one another, Djuna now understands, is narcissistic;
each projects aspects of himself or herself onto the other.

Their stultifying passions are expressed in circular imagery and in musical tonalities. Djuna soon grows aware of the dichotomy existing between her father's outer countenance and the weakly structured inner man, and concomitantly she realizes the schism existing within her own psyche. Important too is her growing understanding of the fact that her father is as much her creation as she is his. The illusion she has been harboring concerning her father's "perfectibility" vanishes and she sees him for what he is. When she leaves Valescure, she is no longer bound to her father, but has grown detached. "Today she held the coat of a dead love."

In *The Voice*, Djuna is a lay analyst residing at the Hotel Chaotica in New York. The Voice, whom she consults to heal the breach within her, is a psychoanalyst. He tells her that her detachment, aloofness, and introversion prevent her from participating in life. Case histories are related in the narrative about a lesbian violinist corroded with guilt; about a cellist, Mischa, whose hand is paralyzed and foot crippled; and about a sensual *femme fatale*, Lilith, who is not in love with her husband. Each patient is a facet of Djuna's personality, incarnated, vibrant, weighty. As Djuna's understanding of the roles she is portraying increases, she becomes less and less dependent on the Voice, a kind of father confessor, healer, shaman, and priest image. He, on the other hand, yearns to be accepted by her not merely as a spiritual guide but as a man as well; consequently he loses his authority over Djuna. The volume concludes with a dream Djuna has: she attempts to push a landlocked boat back into the sea.

In both *Winter of Artifice* and *The Voice*, dream and reverie and the stream-of-consciousness technique are fused, no longer with the surrealistic spontaneity and automatism as in *House of Incest*, but rather in the style of Virginia Woolf and James Joyce. The question now is not merely how to enter the protagonists' unconscious and create another inner dimension and logic; the question is now how to use the discerning power of the artist as an instrument capable of sorting out the flow of emerging images and sensations and of sifting and cutting and polishing them in order to create a finished work of art.

Also important here is Nin's preoccupation with the space/time continuum. In the manner of Proust she examines the conflicts that emerge from her struggle between linear and cyclical time schemes as well as between subject and object. Like Proust also, acting as the demiurge throughout, she includes in her antinovelettes hypnopompic and hypnagogic dream sequences that further break up the narration, disrupt the protagonists' dialogues and moods, and uproot their dependency on other individuals and their identifications.

Stylistically speaking, Nin's prose is straightforward. "Conscious order. Excision of irrelevant details"[2] is necessary, she wrote in her *Diary*. Her eidetic imagery is condensed, decanted, and bone hard: "I hate stuffing" (p. 328). What remains is the Giacometti-like statue, the "pure essence of the personality . . . the deepest self."[3]

Stream-of-Consciousness and the Time Factor

The dream taught me not only the delight of sensory images, but the fact, far more vital, that they led directly into this realm of the unconscious which Joyce, Woolf, Proust attained in various ways—Joyce by free association with words, play on words, Proust by trusting the free associative process of memory and staying lingeringly in the realm between sleep and waking which resembles the waking dream, Virginia Woolf by accepting the vision of the poet as reality.[4]

Like Woolf, Nin used poetic and symbolic means to penetrate the inner being, to evoke mood, and to arouse sensations of pain, joy, of love. Both women drew almost exclusively from their own experiences to create the substance for their novels and antinovelettes. Woolf's childhood delineates for the most part the intellectual and leisured upper-middle class. Her descriptions of these people are ambiguous and impressionistic, and her characters are never whole; rather, they live through the actions and reactions of others. The same is true of the characters in *Winter of Artifice* and *The Voice*. Djuna and her father merge and separate as entities, each projecting on the other, each concretizing his or her illusions, phantasmagoria, tensions, and inhibitions. The philosopher George Berkeley suggested "to be perceived is to be." Such a view could be applied to the creatures of Woolf and Nin. Djuna's Don Juan father, with his stiff, unbending outer image and strong, virile countenance, existed for Djuna as an incarnated abstraction throughout her childhood and adolescence. In *The Voice*, though disembodied for the most part, her father is equally present, haunting, absorbing, and wistful.

Woolf was said to have used the Pointillist technique in *The Waves*, which enabled her to add another dimension to her peceptions: a *niveau océanique*. She explored the unknown through clusters of dots. Impressions thus became a conglomerate of separate identities, individual sensations, atomized feelings that took on objective reality when gathered into a cohesive whole. Like Seurat in his painting *La grande jatte*, where masses of intensely colored dots were set out like impersonal "building blocks" in the construction of a unified picture, Nin built up her characters in a series of mobile atoms. Her father, as opposed to the Voice, and Djuna, as contrasted to Lilith, were single entities, disparate forces molded together in an integrated and rigorously planned harmony of personalities. Each was a blending of many clusters of particles, like figures and objects featured in the Pointillist paintings of Seurat, Pissarro, and Signac.

The stream-of-consciousness technique is used to convey each character's psychic life and allows for the presentation of thoughts, impressions, and feelings on a preverbal level, the author remaining aloof, not commending or judging the actions. Woolf used the stream-of-consciousness technique to articulate an entire chemistry of impressions and sensations, from the acidulous to the mellifluous. In *Winter of Artifice* and *The Voice* father and daughter, as well as psychoanalyst and patient, present their fluid and shifting feelings and reactions in free association, symbol motifs, repetition of words, and rhythmic devices. Facts and situations are not as significant as are the notions of *becoming*, of creation, and the flux of being. By using the stream-of-consciousness technique, Nin gives the reader the impression of experiencing two worlds concomitantly: linear time in the conscious frame of reference and the cyclical time scheme as the unconscious pursues its lucid course. The protagonists—as well as the reader—know that time is passing, that moods and feelings must be apprehended instantly if life in all of its fullness is to emerge. Important too is the complex set of relationships that comes into being when using the stream-of-consciousness technique: the past, present, and future of each of the protagonists is fluid and as such flows into an eternal time scheme. Characters are presented as sharply delineated impressions that then become reflected and refracted, thus interacting upon one another; each penetrating the other's world, diffused, disparate; each a luminosity with its own aerial transparency, its own earthly yearnings.

Neither Woolf's nor Nin's protagonists are active in the sense that they seek exterior adventure like Sterne's Tristram Shandy does or Fielding's Tom Jones. Woolf and Nin prefer introverted beings who probe, think, meditate, reflect. Their characters use interior monologues to convey their visions in ordered sequences; that is, they use their own logic, which may set up mysterious resonances and correspondences in the reader. In Woolf's *To the Lighthouse*, the warmth of the protagonists as they indulge in their human relations is achieved through the repetition of a phrase that resonates like a refrain throughout the work, each time pointing up the tenderness and delicacy of the mood. The same may be said of *Winter of Artifice* and *The Voice*; for example, the words "mask," "rhythm," "time," and "circular" are repeated in many different ways, each time underscoring the artificiality, the hypocrisy, the struggle involved. The mystery of mood and of beings is incubated and its secrets revealed in droplets, particles, aromas, liquid experiences, a blend of visual and sensual motifs.

Joyce used the stream-of-consciousness technique and free association in depicting the thoughts and feelings of his characters. Rather than recounting linear events, which he considered artificial and unlike life, he follows his characters' unconscious yearnings and emotions, allowing some to reveal their multiple points of view and conflicts. In *Ulysses*, Molly Bloom expresses her thoughts helter-skelter at night when serene after having made love. The unconscious flow of memories and reveries that emerges portrays her better and more realistically than any kind of expressionistic description. She takes on life: an undifferentiated woman who lives on an instinctual dimension where tactile forces predominate and sensuality reigns supreme. Similarly, Nin allows Djuna to speak out from subliminal spheres, either in a state of repose or in a frenzied state of anguish, and each time emotions bubble forth uninhibited and uninterrupted until the power energizing her articulations slackens. Every time Djuna allows free association or stream-of-consciousness to take hold, the reader is better able to understand her torment and her feelings of incarceration or paralysis.

Proust's influence on Nin was as significant as Woolf's and Joyce's, perhaps more so with regard to the concept of time. *Winter of Artifice*, Nin wrote, "was a struggle with shadows,"[5] that is, a fight against time, its shifting relationships, its harmonizations and discords. In both of Nin's antinovelettes the protagonists recapture and relive ideal relationships that existed only in their fantasy worlds—in imagined Edenic periods. Proust's intent was, of course, different. He resurrected a past he had loved and without which he could no longer live. In *Remembrance of Things Past* he tried to restore a period when he had been the focal point of his mother's life. Until her death, Proust had known only perfect maternal love: a doting mother who hovered over her son's needs and desires, who tried to alleviate the severity of his asthmatic attacks, but who might have been unwittingly their cause. When she died, Proust wrote (at the age of 34), "She takes my life away with her."

Unlike Proust's past, Djuna's was not wonderful. Yet, in her mind's eye, there were moments of ecstasy during those early years when she and her family traveled together from one exciting experience to another: concerts, hotels, fame, fortune, luxury, parties. There were other moments, however, and these grew more prolonged, when recriminations, insults, anger, and war invaded the household. Also her father denigrated her intellectually and physically. She felt shattered. Djuna did not want to re-create the past; she wanted to create one.

The past, Henri Bergson once said, lives in every individual, conserved in its every detail, such as feelings, thoughts, longings. Frequently, the individual may be unaware of the storehouse of treasures that lives within him, which Bergson called "captured duration." Proust used Bergson's concepts of time and space as a literary device that he related to memory. Memory is divided into two categories: voluntary and involuntary. Voluntary memory when associated with time, destroys everything in the world including civilizations. Man is powerless to stop the present from transforming itself into the past and the future into the present. When the subject, who is no longer young, returns to his childhood home, he finds that everything has changed. People erode as do material objects; they age, disintegrate, and die—and so do feelings of love and hate. Relationships are not static entities. A person may be viewed in one way at one point in life, and in another way years later. The "I" is always shifting; soul states alter; needs and interests transform.

Involuntary memory, on the other hand, when associated with time, restores an internalized past into a present reality that voluntary memory cannot achieve. The mind and body, Proust maintained, are "receptacles" of time and experience. And in the form of "privileged moments," time can be resurrected through any of the five senses. The narrator in *Remembrances of Things Past*, for example, as a young man lived in Paris. He returned to his home one cold winter afternoon and his mother served him tea and cakes called *petites madeleines*. No sooner had the young man sipped some tea and placed a piece of cake in his mouth than he "shuddered." Something extraordinary had happened within him: "A delicious pleasure had invaded me, isolated, without any notion of its cause . . . I stopped feeling mediocre, contingent, mortal." An entire segment of his past had floated into the present and well-being invaded him. He was reliving those Sunday mornings as a child in the country at his aunt's house, when she had given him tea and madeleines. His past existed in the present—active, energetic, delightful. Time had been recaptured because it had never died; it had been incorporated within him.

Reality, or linear time, was for Proust deceiving and superficial. The layers of past experiences—that "immense edifice of souvenir"—added depth to his existence. However, to rely too greatly on *simultaneity of sensation*, which paves the way for involuntary recall as in the incident above, Proust warned, is to allow oneself to become dependent upon chance. It is through the network of art that the revelation of the inner man may be recorded for eternity. When the writer experiences involuntary memory, he must apprehend these moments and fix the insights with the help and concordance of the rational mind. To Proust the work of art was so powerful a force that it took on the importance of a religion. It had its sacred rituals during which time the writer could experience "supraterrestrial" joy. For Proust the artist was a priest, a master of ceremonies, a psychopomp, and a shaman who understood the initiatory procedures that grant eternity.

In her own way Nin too recaptured segments of the

past in *Winter of Artifice* and in *The Voice*. Simultaneity
of sensations enabled her to re-create an atmosphere and
a mood she had experienced twenty years previously, in
a hotel room at Valescure, when her father's cold and arro-
gant air dazzled and terrified her. Nin's analysts also helped
her bring up her past, which she incarnated in the various
protagonists that filled the Hotel Chaotica. In *The Voice* it
is the "friction of the words" that arouses Djuna's involuntary memory sequences, bringing turmoil and pain, mystery
and yearning. Like her mentor Proust, Nin captured secret
relationships through subtle metaphors or through suggestion, revealing all the while hidden analogies, clusters of
intuitions, and conduits leading to various levels of existence. And like Proust, Nin not only experienced the feelings
resurrected but also analyzed, dissected, and objectified them
in turn, as though observing specimens through a micro-
scope—generating and regenerating creatures in an endless
death-rebirth ritual.

Winter of Artifice

Although the patriarchal world order dominates in
"Winter of Artifice," as it does in *House of Incest*, a new
note is sounded: Djuna is not helpless and passive. She is
aware of her fantasies and illusions, the world she has created, and seeks a new orientation. But first she must be certain of the existing state of affairs. She must experience her
father's presence again, his world, as an adult. Only then will
she be able to understand the distorted picture of her father
she bears within her since childhood.

The symbol used to depict the narrator's soul states—
her progressive detachment from her father and the creation
of her own destiny—is encapsulated in an image delineated
at the outset of *Winter of Artifice*; the bowl and the glass
fish within, which may have been inspired by Matisse's series
of paintings of goldfish in a bowl (1915). "This glass bowl
with the glass fish and the glass ship—it has been the sea for

her and the ship which carries her away from him after he
had abandoned her."

Nin was playing with an optical illusion; goldfish in
water, and particularly when made of glass, reflect and re-
fract light, and thus twist the objects out of shape. The
curved bowl further distorts the original image of the fish
within. Forms, then, although distinct, become misshapen;
although clear, become blurred.

Such are Djuna's sensations when seeing her father
after many years of absence. The fishbowl contains its objects: they are incarcerated, yet protected from breakage or
other malevolent forces; that the fish are of glass indicates
their hardness and brittleness as well as their immobility.
Although glass is transparent, it acts as a separation: the fine
wall existing between father and daughter, between outer
and inner worlds. Djuna at times experiences her father as a
glass object—an unbending and brittle entity. For this reason, perhaps, she can see through him and perceive him in a
variety of poses, circumstances, moods, and reflections.
"People were made of crystal for her. She could see right
through their flesh, through and beyond the structure of
their bones" (p. 93).

Fish represent psychic life, nourishment, and a potential world. Pisces, the last sign of the zodiac before rebirth,
symbolizes the world of the spirit existing beyond the world
of appearances. Fish and ships flow through waters and have
been associated in this regard with mystic entities: "ship of
life," or the Egyptian sun god's "night sea journey," which is
undertaken in a boat.

During the confrontation with her father, Djuna on one
occasion leans backward and inadvertently pushes "the
crystal bowl against the wall." It cracked and the "water
gushed forth as from a fountain, spilling all over the floor."
Disruption and disorientation. A breakage has taken place.
"The glass ship could no longer sail away—it was lying on
its side, on the rock-crystal stones" (p. 69). The narrator

bemoans the fact that the fish-ship (now the image is fused) cannot budge: the ship lies on its side, dying for lack of water, starving for nutrients. What Djuna does not know yet is that the fish heretofore enclosed in the bowl are also dying, unable to flow or float—unable to shape events, to function in life, to orient destiny.

The shattered bowl is a step forward and can be looked upon as a step in Djuna's evolution. Her energy is no longer imprisoned in the glass bowl. It has been shattered and scattered. Should another image not be forthcoming, however, such a dispersion of being and evaporation of water and spirit could lead to death.

Glass, as we have seen, acts as a division, a compartmentalization of inner and outer personalities. Djuna's father has a dual personality: his persona, or mask, functions as a mediating complex and is visible in company, during concert tours, or when he wants to seduce women. By donning the mask he effects a compromise personality that enables him to mediate between himself (the individual) and the society (collective) whose admiration he needs. The mask allows him to stand above others, particularly above members of his family. But with the mask he rejects the individual world in favor of the collective. It strengthens the breach between the outer and inner man. His persona, with which his ego identifies at times, leads to a state of inflation. Imbued with self-admiration, he speaks on occasion in lofty tones with pride at being the great concert virtuoso and the handsome, elegant Don Juan. "When he was not smiling, his face was a Greek mask, his blue eyes enigmatic, the features sharp and wilful" (p. 70). At other times, his weak inner self protrudes. His self-esteem deflated, he complains and indulges in self-pity. Arriving at the hotel with Djuna, for instance, he complains of excruciating pain. "He was cursing his lumbago." He can hardly move; yet he will not allow his daughter to help him unpack his valise. He wants no intimacy; people must be kept at a distance so he can hide the weakly structured Don Juan he really is. There he is in all his glory—unable to bend or stand, looking grotesque, ridiculous, pusillanimous.

The man behind the mask is constantly struggling with his outer self. This conflict is manifested in various ways: his obsessive cleanliness, his orderliness, the rigidity of his attitudes. "His clothes were never wrinkled, he wore clean linen every day and his fur collar on his coat was wonderful to caress. He was always immaculate, elegant, sweet smelling, strong, handsome" (p. 60). The inner man is fearful, timid, almost feminine—a pitiful aging Don Juan. Because of his inability to adapt to society—to reveal himself as he is instead of hiding behind his persona—he is a solitary figure divested of everything that is real, alive, and moving. He opts for an imaginary and abstract realm: a fantasy world he has created. What remains behind the impenetrable mask is a feeble and unrelated being.[6]

Djuna's father never analyzes himself and never attempts to know himself. He functions as an automaton hiding behind his mask. For Djuna, at times he is cold and unreachable, a remote figure who has refused to acknowledge her as an individual and considers her only as a love object or as someone from whom he seeks to escape. "His face wore a mask. The skin did not match the skin of his wrists" (p. 67), Djuna notes as she begins to see her father more objectively. Neither guilt nor self-hate plague him. His centroversion is such that nothing matters except the gratification of his desires.

Djuna begins to notice the severe split that exists within him: the outer being that tries to live up to the image people have created of him, and the inner being that is flabby, weak, effeminate. The greater the breach between the inner and outer man and the more emotional and quixotic his behavior becomes, the more tragic a figure he is. Djuna has experienced him in many of his roles. When she was a child, he represented perfection, but he could also be insulting, belittling, or terrifying. The only time calm existed was when guests arrived. Then the persona dominated. Djuna experienced her father as a destructive force: a negative god image with mythological ramifications.

Her father was standing behind a window, watching. There was never a smile on his face except when there were visitors, except when there was music and talk. When they were alone in the house there was always war: great explosions of anger, hatred, revolt. War. . . . A life rippled with dissension.
     Her father's eyes were always cold, critical, unbelieving. Because he was so critical, so severe, so suspicious of her, she became secretive and lying. . . . (pp. 57, 58)

On the other hand, he was also a positive god figure. "Her true God was her father. At communion it was her father she received, and not God" (p. 65).
     The father-daughter identification is close. Each projects contents of his unconscious onto the other. He becomes an extension of her personality and she of his. She is his anima figure (inner woman), and he her animus (inner man). In both cases the attitudes are unconscious; images encapsulate characteristics the conscious attitude lacks. Proust once suggested that love is a projection; what is of import, however, is the depth of such a projection.
     At the outset of *Winter of Artifice*, Djuna lives in a state of virtual identification with her father, as the initial image of the fishbowl indicates. She is imprisoned in her father's vision of her and hers of him. But as long as she experiences her father as a judge or critic whose persistent eye observes her every action, she will not be free to live her own life. "It was as if behind her there stood a judge, a tall judge he alone could see, and to this judge her father addressed a beautiful polished speech . . ." (p. 68). At other moments, the animus offers her delight. "But she was so happy to have found a father, a father with a strong will, a wisdom, an infallible judgment, that she forgot for the moment everything she knew, surrendered her own certainties" (p. 80). To have a father who is seer and God answers,

at least for the moment, her needs. Yet, when functioning in the real world, she realizes that his overly critical demeanor hounds her (his voice constantly reverberates in her ear drum), cuts her off from her own feminine nature, and shatters her—symbolized in the fishbowl image.

As long as Djuna does not create some kind of connection or real relationship with a positive animus figure, she will not be able to experience an authentic rapport with a man. When feeling harassed or defeated, she would escape; if surfeited with attention, she would grow bored; reviled by a man, she would feel ugly and lacking in harmony. She would blame herself for being unable to fulfill her role as woman. The animus acts upon her like a *daemon*.

In time Djuna begins to evaluate her situation. She sees other aspects of her father that allow her to wrench herself away from him. The identification or *participation mystique*, that made of her a dependent nature, is now being severed. When, for example, her father reads her diary and discovers that she has had a life of her own and made friends of her own and has not spent twenty years mourning a father who deserted the family, his jealousy and anger are aroused. He feels Djuna is leaving him as other women in his life, including his second wife, have left him. The aging Don Juan that becomes visible is to her pitiful, and she does not see herself any more as the "mystical bride of her father" or as floating about blindly in the nebulous area between illusion and reality.

Beneath the handsome countenance, the romantic and glittering concert pianist who played in every capital in Europe before captivated audiences, another individual is exposed: a man in the prime of life, who has not yet awakened to the realities of the world. Because he cannot understand or face himself, he is unable to develop a higher consciousness and is caught off balance by Djuna. Not able to accept his limitations, he is given to outbursts of rage in situations with which he cannot cope. The overly immaculate and rigid man is his own antagonist, his own destroyer.

Djuna's awakening ego causes her to begin paying attention to her own needs and desires, to fulfill herself and not live any more as a reflection or projection. Thus she finds it unnecessary to play the role she had thought would please her father and which he expects of her.

The musical image interwoven into the narrative at this juncture in a stream-of-consciousness sequence acts as a conclusion to the first step of Djuna's separation process. To choose music as a demarcation line indicates that music, and the feeling associated with it, is the vehicle required to pass onto another stage of Djuna's development. Her father tells her that, just as music remains indefinable and amorphous, so the women in his life are "incognito." When he thinks about his women, he says, "it comes out a *do* or a *la*, and who could recognize them in a sonata?" (p. 69). It is this inability to see women as individuals that prevents him from coming to terms with them or with himself. Interesting in this work is the fact that a musician makes analogies in a way similar to alchemists, who associate metals with planets and personalities. *Fa, do, sol* are considered masculine elements and associated with fire and air; *la, mi, ti* are feminine and pertain to water and earth. It is significant, then, that the father explains, "it comes out a do or a la," which indicates an unconscious yearning to perform a marriage between opposites—that is, between fire and air (symbolized by *do*) and earth and water (symbolized by *la*). This points up the feminine and masculine components within his personality: the inner and outer man, or strength and weakness.

For Nin, as well as Proust, musical tones had a literary equivalent. As emotions can be articulated and translated into another language, so melody can be formulated into the word. Proust used to go to the Salle Pleyel in Paris and listen to Beethoven quartets; or he would ask his friend Reynaldo Hahn to play and sing for him; and sometimes he hired musicians to come to his house. Proust felt it was not sufficient to convey sensations through analogy; they had to be materialized and explicated for the reader. Like Plato's

"Allegory of the Cave," music may be looked upon as a series of constructs, clusters of shadows, and resonances that the composer intuits, interprets, and then recaptures in fleeting tones and shifting rhythms. Art preserves the sense experience.

For both Nin and Proust, music represents an emotional involvement. They each associate melodies, harmonies, and rhythms with some situation, relationship, or feeling. Djuna experiences an orchestrated interlude with her father, "as if they were listening to music . . . inside both their heads . . . there was a concert going on." The image is grandiose: an orchestra composed of a hundred instruments. The violin is singled out for scrutiny and compared to nerves: "and she passing the violin bow gently between her legs; drawing music out of her body . . . " (p. 85). For Djuna, the violin represents the heart: gentle, tender, and suffering. Other instruments express the personalities of father and daughter: the vibrating drums with their rhythms, tone, timbre, and serial patterns incorporate the syncopated beats of the soul, the mystical correspondences between the individual and the universe at large. Pythagorean "music of the spheres," dependent upon meter and number, also represents a melodic hierarchy of emotions. The high-pitched tones of the violin represent a leap of anguish; the brass, strings, and timpani express in loud and subdued vibrations the moods of repose and terror.

Music has been called "the science of modulations." In many civilizations, during traumatic periods, music is used as a mediating force between God and man. When Orpheus played his harmonies, he hypnotized his listeners (inanimate as well as animate) into submission. Djuna, a disciple of Orpheus, sought out her master's way: she drank from the waters of Mnemosyne (memory) in the underworld, or inner world; not from the waters of Lethe, which lead to forgetfulness. In the land of memory she is able to conjure up a past that helps her distinguish truth from fiction and so pass onto the next stage of her development. "No music could come from the orchestra" when her father conducted it, she now realizes. He was too rigid, submerged in detail and structure—in outer, not inner tonalities.

The glass bowl and the musical interlude enable Djuna to understand and successfully pass to the third step of her growth process. As she and her father are driving south, he takes off his shoe because it is too tight. When he

pulled off his sock she saw the foot of a woman. It was delicate and perfectly made, sensitive and small. She felt as if he had stolen it from her: it was her foot she was looking at, her foot he was holding in his hand. She had the feeling that she knew this foot completely. It was her foot—the very same size and the very same color, the same blue veins showing and the same air of never having walked at all. (p. 91)

The foot is a catalyst. It forces her to regress. She looks upon it as hers, a double. The identification is so great that she loses all ability to differentiate. What is hers? Her self-estrangement is apparent, her facelessness disconcerting. Father and daughter are now pathologically linked. Had such a condition continued, Djuna would never have been born into womanhood. Her task, she knows, is to dissociate herself from her father. That the foot should be the instrument to effect such a severing is significant. Feet represent one's relationship with the earth principle: the foot contacts the earth physically. It is at opposite poles with the head, spirit, and soul. Yet, it is linked to the so-called higher being. One without the other cannot function harmoniously. The foot is also a phallic symbol, and the removal of the shoe a feminine element. Thus is the mask removed from both father and daughter.

Djuna singles out the foot for observation because she is ready to step out of her old existence as her father's reflection and appendage. She is beginning to adapt—naked—to the world at large. No mask is necessary. Certainly her father has wronged her by his egotism and negativity. But the daughter likewise prolonged this infantile and unfortunate rapport. She could not yet extricate herself from her dependency on the patriarchal image. At times she attempts to be what she thinks he wanted her to be: beautiful, charming, delectable—an anima figure. At other times, she rebels. She resents not being herself and is determined to cast him off. Like the shoe, he cramped her style, restricted her movement, the pain became unbearable.

At the conclusion of *Winter of Artifice*, Djuna "held the coat of a dead love" before her and the nightmare as she has known it is over. She refuses to be the little girl, the cripple suffering from remorse and guilt. She seeks to transform herself into a mature woman. As such, she does not need a father. The patriarchal society she has experienced, with its negative father image, could not help her find fulfillment.

The Voice

Just as the bowl of goldfish contains the germ of *Winter of Artifice*, so the early image of Djuna lying in her "cell-shaped room" in the Hotel Chaotica reveals the underlying themes of *The Voice* (p. 120). The Hotel Chaotica, like the fishbowl, is a microcosm. It is filled with living beings that struggle, love, and hate in an attempt to keep alive amid insurmountable difficulties. Because the action takes place in New York, Nin chose to dramatize the events in *crescendo* and at a *prestissimo* pace. The condition created by people disgorging from the elevators, messengers rushing about, telegrams and mail being delivered, and phones ringing is one of turmoil and disquietude. The rhythms and cacophonies are high-powered, frenetic, and act like clusters of catalysts.

At first the Voice, which is the psychoanalyst, is disembodied. Djuna therefore is no longer talking with her flesh-and-blood father but rather with a sublimated, spiritual being—a collective figure, healer, shaman—who is helping Djuna to "be born again." His method requires regression.

He wants Djuna to turn back to her childhood so that through her talk he will be able to pinpoint her trauma and understand the split corroding her psyche. "I want to reconcile you to yourself," he says (p. 122).

As in the case of spiritual figures such as oracles, deities, and heroes in ancient times, the Voice emerges from a cavelike, or cell-like, area clothed in darkness. The containing factor of the room gives Djuna a feeling of protection and security resembling the warm and understanding uterine inner world. She begins to feel at ease. Far from the crowd and the masks she has to don, removed from the lies of life's experience and the hurt that has caused her such pain, Djuna is able to withdraw into herself and experience her "dark night of the soul"—her Orphic descent. Within these quiet inner recesses she listens to the Voice and experiences the patriarchal force as a saving spirit, a kind of God, as in the Gospel of St. John (1): "In the beginning was the Word, and the Word was with God, and the Word was God." The Voice is her God, an impersonal force and a positive spirit that brings her torment, to be sure, but also innundates her world with energy sufficiently powerful to disentangle the knots that paralyze her existence. Like the mystic, she reaches out to the Voice in articulate terms and expresses her moments of ecstatic joy in a past that surges forth to become a present reality. Past and present weave their way throughout the narrative in syncopated rhythms and energetic patterns, clearing and cleansing an encumbered existence.

The visual image is that of a series of instantaneous snapshots. Emotions and sensations are caught and fixed in a unique instant, each harboring secret selves, each revealing countless treasures and arcana. Djuna still shuns the outside world. She seeks to remain in the darkness of her cell-like room of the hotel that is an integrated image of her baroque inner world. Like an animal that has been maligned and hurt throughout life, she slinks into her introspective world. The Voice seeks her out and assuages her pain. He commands her to look outward to the stream of people in the hall and into the world beyond the hotel.

As in Samuel Beckett's play *Not I*, which features a mouth as a protagonist, so the Voice narrates his diagnosis: Djuna does not participate in life; she stands still and has cut herself off from the mainstream. Djuna remonstrates. She observes the outside world, the stream of people being "carried away," not one master of his or her destiny. Chance, automatism, flux. Obsessed with the fleeting nature of time, she comments, people are like "debris." Destruction is implicit in the human as well as in the organic object. Djuna has not yet adapted to life, nor has she been transformed by it. Time is experienced as eschatological, not as a cyclical force; therefore clock time pervades. She feels the fleeting nature of past, present, and future; anguish pervades her being: her fear of getting old, of dying without having made one's imprint on the world. She articulates her mistakes, pains, and suffering in a series of fragmented phrases that float about in contradictory and antithetical images as elements in space. Each phrase when uttered seems to be caught up in another network of abrasive, searing visualizations. Time is experienced as destructive. It is as devisive a force as Djuna herself. Each aspect of her personality tears at the other; nothing works in harmony. Djuna knows only temporal consciousness but not the feeling of eternity. Her life is as cut up as time divided into seconds, minutes, days, weeks, months, years.

Along with her emotional fragmentation as envisaged through time, Djuna is bombarded by rhythms and floating forms that invade her cell-shaped room. She finally takes the Voice's advice and forces her way out of her room into the street and thus into collective existence. A reduction of distance between herself and the world at large takes place—a confrontation. She feels compelled to deal with reality now that she is beyond the safety of her walled room and hotel. She must fight for survival: "moving, moving. Flowing, flowing, flowing" (p. 124). The repetition of words and phrases is caught up in a network of fleeting images. Djuna remains powerless and immovable, as if experiencing a non-verbal zone: wordless visualizations are reproduced as if in a dream. Contrapuntal beats intrude and project themselves onto objects around her, radiating outward into some distant area, some future time-space continuum. Music interweaves its tonalities into the instant, resuscitates past moods. "No days without music. She is like an instrument so tuned up, so exacerbated, that without hands, without players, without leadership, it responds, it breathes, it omits the continuous melody of sensibility. Never knew silence" (p. 152).

Speed increases, dilates, and intensifies. As in a Futurist painting, Djuna portrays her inner dynamism in successive stages of motion and emotion, movement and life. Like the canvases of Severini and Boccioni, which suggest motion by cutting up heretofore single forms, so Djuna attempts to cope with her feelings of frustration by an inner dismemberment. Then, as she examines each aspect of her inner being, she projects frequently on the world outside of herself; she fuses with the beings on the crowded and cluttered street, with the machines speeding by; with objects of all types. Like a sculpture, she becomes a prolongation of space. She feels energized and transformed by the speeding forces at work. As in Marcel Duchamp's painting *Nude Descending a Staircase* (1912), she experiences an inner destruction and the loss of her ego amid the stifling and crushing collective forces.

I have the fear that everyone is leaving, moving away, that love dies in an instant. I look at the people walking in the street, just walking, and I feel this: they are walking, *but* they are also being *carried away*. They are part of a current. . . . I confuse the moods which change and pass with the people themselves. I see them carried into eddies, always moving out of some state they will never return to. I see them lost (p. 123).

Parallel images surface. With slight alterations Nin created a link between *Winter of Artifice* and *The Voice*:

musical tonalities emerge and inject a sense of liberation, an unheard-of freedom. The shoe-and-foot image in *Winter of Artifice* is recaptured in *The Voice*, but viewed in a different way. When Djuna, for example, is speaking to the Voice, she removes her shoes to "uncover her very small and delicate feet" (p. 116). The atmosphere is now feminized. She knows that she is alluding to *her* foot and to no one else's. No longer a projection, a fantasy image, or a fetish, the foot stands for her rapport with reality. But minutes later a nebulous world imposes its presence and contradictory images abound; a series of isolated visualizations, as if suspended in space, come into being in the conversation between Djuna and the Voice.

A succession of characters comes into focus: Hazel, Georgia, Lilith, Mischa—each a projection of Djuna. Scenes catapult forth and these incarnations impress their personalities onto the proceedings; recognition and cognition come into being. Lilith, a lesbian violinist, feels the weight of her guilt to such an extent that she cannot play any more. The Voice heals her. Mischa, the cripple who cannot play his cello because his hand has grown stiff, after consulting the Voice begins to accept his problems and adapt to them.

Djuna returns to the lobby of the Hotel Chaotica. Her foray into the external world, the street, has seared her. "Her throat tightened." Yet, each time she has to face life within the hotel, she is equally terror stricken. She fears that "*someone out of the past*" (p. 135) will emerge and she will be unable to cope with the instincts and emotions that may surge forth. She fears to be reminded of her youth and her adolescence. Her inner world, ablaze and cut open by conflicting instincts and emotions, is expressed by discordant metaphors that now haunt the narrative. Spatial and temporal incongruities seem to sever what should have been whole and seem to disorder what should have been channeled. Unlike Proust's narrator, who enjoyed the upsurging of past sensations, Djuna dreads it. She thought she had thrown out her past "with the broken toys, but they sat there, threatening to sweep her back" (p. 135). They stand undaunted within her mind's eye like broken-faced gargoyles: "stuffed, with glass eyes, from a slower world, they look at her on this other level of swifter rhythms until they reach with dead arms around her" (p. 135). Djuna feels suspended in some airy sphere and contemplates the world about her: its tangled emotions, its discarded feelings. The drama unfolds: from the window in her room she sees a woman committing suicide by jumping out of a window. Although the psychological implication of such an image implies that an aspect of Djuna seeks suicide, we know that she seeks desperately to maintain some kind of balance amid the disruptive instincts invading her. The crippling effects of the images that emerge helter-skelter from the inner world are taking their toll as they vibrate, titillate, and shock her into a new state of awareness. Djuna does not wish to escape any more. Slowly, ploddingly, she goes on to the next step of *gnosis*: her own development.

That Lilith should play a role in *Winter of Artifice* is significant. The original Lilith as introduced in Talmudic literature was Adam's first wife. She was a harlot, adamant in her desire to captivate and hold men within her grasp. Unable to bear children and with no milk in her breasts, her aim was to divest other mothers of their newborns. Slim and beautiful with wings and the feet of an owl, Lilith was forever seducing men, revenging herself upon them for her own deficiencies.[7] Lilith is an aspect of Djuna. She is that part of Djuna that seeks to dominate the patriarchal world. She is Lilith the demon, the nymphomaniac who seeks to attract, seduce, and then destroy her victim. She is the female Don Juan.

Lilith works her magic on the Voice. But as long as he remains remote—the seer, the God, the father—he holds dominion over her. When at the end of the story he becomes humanized and incorporates the frailties incumbent on a corporeal man, that is, when he longs to be loved as a man rather than as a deity, her idealization of him vanishes. "In the Voice she felt the ugliness of tree roots, of the earth, and this terrific dark, mute knowing of the animal" (p. 164). She wants spirit, but he seeks the flesh.

What she read in his eyes was the immense pleading of a man, imprisoned inside a seer, calling out for the life in her, and at the very moment when every cell inside her body closed to the desire of the man she saw a mirage before her . . . a figure taller than other men, a type of savior, the man nearest to God, whose human face she could no longer see except for the immense hunger in the eyes. (p. 163)

The real man, whether father or psychoanalyst, could not capture her being. Only the sublimated, spiritual force could invade her soul.

Winter of Artifice concludes with a premonitory dream. It reveals in images Djuna's inability to cope with her still fragmented world, her longing for orientation, her desire to escape into the ineffable world of reverie where she can experience her narcissism to her heart's content. It also shows her feverish desire to face herself, to succeed as woman and artist.

"When I entered the dream I stepped on stage" (p. 170). She is actress and observer. She prepares for her exciting venture into the fourth dimension—time. The vertical and the horizontal mark her course: "a tower of layers without end, rising upward and closing themselves in the infinite, or layers, coiling downward, losing themselves in the bowels of the earth." The dreamer explodes, bursts, shatters. She loses her course as she traverses spatial domains. She experiences the void in which potential creation lives. She experiences empty fields, a one-way course. She needs to expand and experience the fullness of life—the mystic's All. The inability to let go and feel her identity, to find her way amid the whirling and spiraling waters and rocking rhythms, terrorizes her. The beats lull the sleeper into a semiconscious state.

A *participation mystique* again comes over Djuna. She

begins feeling one with organic form. She feels herself breathing in the "life of plants" in a flower. She becomes a biomorphic form, a fish, living inorganically, as Lautréamont's character Maldoror. Individuality vanishes. She embraces the cosmos. The collective dominates. She longs for a loss of memory. Her personalities flake and erode as time is measured by the hourglass. She longs for cyclical time—the mystic's celestial sphere. Daybreak and consciousness enter the dream. "The soul then lost its power to breathe, lost its space." Weighed down with the pain of life, divested of her nightly vision, of her anterior existences that had encrusted pain on her braised skin, yet allowed her to know grandiose heights, she clings desperately to some stable force as night descends. Details are blurred. Delineations grow unclear. Individual existences blend into multiple worlds. Oscillation and vibration radiate their ambivalent sensations, multiply and generate excitement, energize her being, arouse her flights of fancy and intensify her need for liberation. "The pressure of time ceased" (p. 173). The most important section of the dream, an image that will be repeated in many of Nin's works, is related:

The boat I was pushing with all my strength because it could not float, it was passing through land. It was chokingly struggling to pass along the streets, it could not find its way to the ocean. It was pushed along the streets of the city, touching the walls of houses, and I was pushing it against the resistance of the earth. So many nights against the obstacles of mud, marshes, garden paths through which the boat labored painfully . . .

The boat was passing through the city unable to find the ocean that transmitted its life voyages. The light cut into the bones with bony words that could not commune or change substance for communion. (p. 174)

Conceived as a microcosm, the ship is associated with maritime and spatial navigation. It is the earthly counterpart of an astral vehicle. In Djuna's dream the ship is not directed by divinity, but by her. As a receptacle and containing device, the boat is associated with the womb, the inner woman. Djuna's ship is landlocked. No matter how hard she tries to push it, to guide it through the cluttered city streets, the marshes, the insurmountable convolutions and involutions of life, it is too heavy for her. Djuna seeks the free-flowing water, the preformal state before birth, without obstacles and difficulties, just floating about without orientation or disorientation. She is impeded in her wish. She must push the boat and she does. Now she relies on no one but herself to find her direction. Neither her father in *Winter of Artifice* nor the Voice are called to participate. Search, struggle, and pain, Djuna is prepared for these eventualities. The artist within her has the will and strength to succeed.

5

oↄ·oↄ·oↄ·oↄ·oↄ·oↄ·oↄ·oↄ·oↄ·oↄ·oↄ·oↄ·oↄ·oↄ·oↄ·oↄ·oↄ·oↄ·oↄ·oↄ·oↄ·oↄ

A Renaissance Artist:
Cities of the Interior

In *Cities of the Interior* (1959), Nin has become a Renaissance artist. No longer the fledgling grasping and floundering about, she is now certain of her course, both literary and psychological, and of the techniques needed to achieve her goal. *Cities of the Interior*, a "continuous novel," includes: *Ladders to Fire* (1946); *Children of the Albatross* (1947); *Four-Chambered Heart* (1950); *A Spy in the House of Love* (1954); *Solar Barque* (1958), which is Part I of the fifth novel of the book; and *Seduction of the Minotaur* (1961), which is Part II of the fifth novel.

As a Renaissance artist, Nin interweaves with great ease the conventions used by the painter and musician with those of the writer. In so doing, she conveys heightened feelings, incarnates an aesthetic, and dramatizes a psychological credo. Conflicts, traumas, and joys are now expressed in tinctures, designs, textures, harmonies, and cacophonies that give a new dimension to *Cities of the Interior*. Inner scapes, although focused upon with microscopic precision in her previous works, are here recounted in dramatic modes. Thus, with the complicity of the pictorial and aural domains, particular characters and special scenes are able to emerge three-dimensionally. Important, too, is the fact that each protagonist is drawn with his "faults" or "foibles" or both; each revolves around a central character like satellites. Symbols are also used three-dimensionally. D. H.

Lawrence once suggested, "symbols don't MEAN something, they ARE units of human experience. And the power of the symbol is to arouse the deep, emotional, dynamic primitive self." It is no wonder that *Cities of the Interior* is a veritable orchestration of the senses that imposes a vast new world upon the reader.

Nin's technique, which some have labeled space fiction, takes the reader out of the mundane world. Similar to the mystic, she sees through the realm of appearance—the masks—directly into her protagonist's biomorphic realm. There, she extracts her materials in the form of fabrics, sounds, and images; then, as with collages, molds and remolds them to suit present moods. Events are viewed as both inner dramas and outer situations, detached and objectified. The reader may thereby study relationships; he may be drawn into them and experience them in rhythmic interchanges, in light-shadow confrontations, or in thrusts and ripostes. Nin's deep psychological acumen and intuitive faculties intensified her power of observation, allowing her to take her stage play out of the personal field of vision and placing it in the mythical. Her characters, now autonomous creations, live out their painful quests and struggle to answer their needs. *Cities of the Interior*, which relates the myth of "the woman at war with herself," activates visceral responses and sets up a new dynamism. To evoke the right touch and quality of feeling, Nin used to read her prose aloud and listen to its reverberations, the impact certain vowels or consonants made upon others as they collided or blended with them. When the right sound was struck, it was noted and the feeling seized upon and brought to life.

Cities of the Interior dramatizes the conflicts involved in the "destruction of women" and "woman's struggle to understand her own nature." Although in modern society, many lived fulfilled lives as mothers, wives, and career women, there are others who are incapable of juggling these roles about and integrating them into their life style. Nin wrote:

. . . many more, when entering action or creation, followed men's pattern and could not carry along or integrate within them the feminine part of themselves. Action and creation, for woman, was man—or an imitation of man. In this imitation of man she lost contact with her nature in her relation to man.[1]

Nin addressed herself to the unfulfilled woman: the pitiful creature who cannot find balance within herself, who rejects what she considers her negative or inferior (shadow) characteristics and experiences, unwittingly perhaps, but nevertheless virtual psychological suicide.

Nin was not the first to write continuous novels. Balzac's *Human Comedy*, for example, is a series of works that form a complete unit: characters appear and depart, each character playing out his life against the backdrop of the society of the period. Zola's "scientific" novels, *The Rougon-Macquart*, may also be said to belong to this category. They depict characters dominated by heredity and environment. In Proust's series, *Remembrance of Things Past*, the narrator is viewed differently by a variety of people from diverse environments.

Nin's continuous novel allowed her to probe her characters in various situations and milieus. These beings, which she labeled "faulty cellular structures," are always in search of wholeness or completion. Each explores the question of whether one person may find completion or liberation in another, "whether through the association of love" one can learn "to be liberated of false values and false roles," whether love can help one create and/or re-create his being.[2]

Although Nin brought her multidimensional world to life through descriptions of concrete objects, it was not the phenomenal world that aroused her interest, it was rather the spiritual experiences.[3] She explained: "I select parts of the external world which reveal the internal, the parts which are necessary to the inner drama. That is what lies behind my seemingly incomplete characters or descriptions of places."[4]

Unlike Nathalie Sarraute, who delineated her characters' inner meanderings by concentrating on tropisms, defined as protoplastic substances that exist between the conscious and unconscious state, Nin took a concrete object and allowed its opacity and its energy to flow forth in feeling tones, thus triggering a complicated network of vibrations and reverberations. Whereas Sarraute indulged in abstractions, thereby dehumanizing her creatures, Nin created characters who live in a very real and worldly environment. In Sarraute's *Tropisms* (1932), *The Portrait of a Man Unknown* (1948), and *The Planetarium* (1959), inner images and rhythms are translated in terms of disintegrating or integrating matter: amoebalike substances that continuously alter in form. Nin's characters are constructed on solid foundations. They are endowed with psychological and physical characteristics, are visible, and are given first names, enabling each in his own way to participate in events, although these may be acausal. Like Sarraute, however, Nin searched for the right image to convey the fleeting sensation and the proper sonority to arouse the impression. Sarraute and Nin were realistic writers and described their visions in natural ways: clothes, decor, objects, feelings; both were also introverted: their worlds centered on the inner domain.

Ladders to Fire

Ladders to Fire[5] is divided into two parts: "This Hunger" and "Bread and the Wafer."

"This Hunger" dramatizes the plight of women who hunger for love, for physical and metaphysical understanding—for wholeness. They are deprived. They live in arid worlds, their appetites are unfulfilled; they wander through life both passively and aggressively, grabbing and holding onto whatever they believe may quench their thirst and placate their needs.

Each of the participating women in *Ladders to Fire* (Stella, Djuna, Sabina, friends of sorts) is a split-off of the central character, Lilian. Each represents an autonomous complex. Because they are fragmented beings, they may be compared to Picasso's *Card Player* (1913) or Braque's *Young Girl with Guitar* (1913), canvases made up of a complex of detached forms. Stella, Djuna, and Sabina are satellite personalities; they live by virtue of Lilian as her mirror reflections. Moreover, the women are symbols, which Nin defined as follows:

The meaning of a symbol can penetrate our unconscious before revealing itself to our conscious intelligence, achieving direct communication as music does, by way of the feelings and the senses. The flexibility of interpretation is an invitation to participate in creation exactly as music demands of us response rather than a rational dissection. It is by this very mobility of interpretation that the living quality is preserved, so that one can *feel* and *experience* a novel rather than read it as one would a detective story, without feeling, as another pastime of the intelligence.[6]

The protagonists are brought to life as personality types, each one representing what Jung defined as a function in the fourfold structure of the psyche: feeling, intuition, thinking, and sensation. Each also personifies an element in accordance with alchemical dicta: air, earth, water, and fire.

Stella lives in a circumscribed environment. She has not yet gone beyond the father-daughter problem delineated dramatically in *Winter of Artifice* and *The Voice*. Stella is a well-known movie star, her father an actor. Like Djuna in the antinovelettes, she has also been deserted by her father. Because of this, she has lost faith in love. The opening image encapsulates the psychological situation: Stella is sitting in "a small, dark room" observing "her own figure acting on the screen." Her stage life is diametrically opposed to her personal world. Her stage personality is nonchalant, positive, self-assured, free and easy, even joyous, captivating in her audience's eyes. Her inner world, on the other hand, is corroded with feelings of self-doubt. This dichotomy re-

veals itself in her love affairs. On the screen or when written
about in magazines, her relationships are profound, dramatic, and marvelously happy. In reality she is so insecure
that she is always demanding proof of her lover's passion for
her. Bruno adores Stella, but "If a telephone call or some
emergency at home tore him away from her, for her it was
abandon, the end of love." She then becomes possessive,
making scenes and indulging in recriminations. In place of
the beautiful and charming screen personality, she is transformed into one who is domineering, devouring. "She must
ravage and conquer the absolute, for the sake of love." She
asks herself why she acts that way; the response, masochism.
Her second love affair with a Don Juan figure fares no better
than the first. She is jealous of her lover's gifts to other
women—gifts he had given before they met. She becomes
angry over his past and forgets to live in the present.

Stella's moods change with the roles she plays. Her
name suits her fragmented personality: outwardly and from
a distance, she is a stellar figure, cold and fearless, light
fighting against darkness and despair, life in conflict with
death. In that stars are visible only at night, only in the
dark room does her collective personality emerge: in the
camera's eye. By day the star has disappeared and Stella, the
woman who feels inferior in every domain, stands forth. "A
fragile Stella, lying in her ivory satin bed, amongst mirrors."[7] Each of her selves is playing havoc with the other.
Each facet of her personality is shattered by the other until
only broken glass remains.

Stella is intuitive and sees into future events. She understands how relationships bloom and then fade into oblivion,
and she is aware of the nature of her malady. But her
insights remain undeveloped, and because they are uncon-
trollable, they frequently lead her astray. When, for example, jealousy flashes into her mind's eye or when she
intuits her lover's slackening interest, her inner visions are
blocked by the pounding fear of solitude and by the death-
dealing experience of rejection she had known so acutely in

childhood. "In her white nightgown she does not look like an enchantress but an orphan," the fatherless daughter, the unwanted woman. "She was a child carrying a very old soul and burdened with it, and wishing to deposit it in some great and passionate role" (p. 45).

As a stellar figure, Stella belongs to the element air. Outwardly, she roams about freely from one land to another, from one film to the next, working long hours, at times frenetically. Inwardly, she is airbound: a slave to her torment, never alighting, never overcoming her sense of inferiority or understanding the depth of the feelings she could arouse in others; and haunted by the thought that men do not love her for herself, but only for "the woman on the screen . . . the face of translucence, the face of wax on which men found it possible to imprint the image of their fantasy." When air is compressed or concentrated, it creates heat or fire. Such were Stella's loves: a series of conflagrations that burned powerfully only to die, smothered from lack of oxygen.

Lilian is a jazz pianist whose powerful personality is associated with the instrument she plays. Hypertense, excitable, constantly in a state of "fermentation," she leaves her children and her husband, who still treats her after ten years of marriage like an adolescent. She longs for adventures— which she has with heterosexuals and homosexuals. Lilian, however, does not experience the hoped-for fulfillment. Gerard, her first lover, sees in her his mother and therefore fears her. Jay, a painter, becomes the *homme fatal* in Lilian's life—her "iron lung." He too considers her a mother figure. Lilian is forever confusing love with sex, and her attitude toward men is defensive. She comes to realize that falling in love for her means projecting onto others disparate facets of her own self. All of her relationships are imprisoning devices and narcissistic. Djuna, Lilian's friend, an orphan brought up in poverty, lives inwardly and rarely displays emotions. She approaches her lovers in a seemingly detached manner. Because "Lilian's femininity was imprisoned in the male Lilian," she thought she could win Djuna's affection by giving her material possessions. Jay's friend Helen arouses Lilian's jealousy, but she soon leaves the scene at Lilian's suggestion.

Lilian is a feeling type and may be associated with the element earth. She never functions as an independent individual, always in terms of others. She rejects the world she has created with her husband and children because she considers it "death," "claustrophobic." When she and her husband used to sit together in the evenings, "he did not appear to see her," she complains. Her husband spells stasis. He spoke of events that had happened years before and lived in a past that no longer existed—in a world devoid of growth. Lilian draws a parallel between her life and a neighbor's whose wife had died six months previously and who had been living with the cadaver "stretched on his bed" ever since. No longer able to stand "the image of death" incised in her world, Lilian opts for life and activity.

Feeling types are prone to extremes of behavior. Highly emotional, their thinking funtion is usually inferior; the capacity to abstract and objectify their relationships is denied them. They evaluate and judge only in terms of how they feel about a person. From the outset Lillian is described as frenetic, volatile, visceral, and excessive.

She was always in full movement, in the center of a whirlpool of people, letters, and telephones. She was always poised on the pinnacle of a drama, a problem, a conflict. She seemed to trapeze from one climax to another, from one paroxysm of anxiety to another, skipping always on the peaceful region in between.

Words such as "galvanized," "boil," "larval," "earthquake," "havoc," are used to depict her flagrant and disruptive personality. In her kitchen, she is delineated in analogies with the cooking process, that transformatory ordeal that changes primitive substances into refined materials. Lilian's archaic psyche, however, concocts a "witches brew," reminiscent of "the sword swallowers at the fair, the fire-eaters and the glass-eaters of the Hindu magic sects," Nin wrote. Spices with all of their tangy, harsh, burning sensations blend into her personality, leaving her smarting after each encounter; yet she pursues her way blindly, like some volcanic force. She is a laboratory of "continuous explosions." Her hyper-sensitive nature follows her everywhere like a series of echoes and hammer beats. The tumult she sets off in the heart and mind of those she meets is not easily extinguished.

Lilian has an anthropoid psyche. It is undeveloped and experiences life on its most primitive level: earth-oriented, Dionysian, solid, physical, strong. She is a throwback to a prelogical being who lives on an instinctual level and who can no more learn from experience than she can from abstraction. Like the primitives, Lilian's sense organs are keen and her earthbound nature allows her to feel into situations incisively. Her lack of judgment, however, permits her impulses to guide her. Rather than think out her animal needs and wants, she remains passive. When her emotional attachments fail to bring her the satisfaction for which she longs, fail to make her feel *whole*, she withdraws into her lair, like a maimed animal, and indulges in self-repudiation, self-hate, and psychological suicide.

A possessed woman unable to see through her problems, blind to her needs and to those of her friends, Lilian's love affairs follow the same patterns, whether heterosexual or homosexual: attraction first, then passion, with fear of loss followed by a need to hold on, possess, and dominate the love object. Feelings of rejection and withdrawal ensue. The birth of a new experience and the scheme of things is re-lived.

Lilian is a mother figure for the men in her life. She enjoys playing this role and is often literally swept off her feet by the power of her sexual impulses. It is no wonder that she frequently dreams of a "ghost lover . . . a pale, passive, romantic, anemic figure." Who else could live with such a volcanic type? Her first lover, Gerard, is "smiling, passive, static" and is described as an "extinct volcano."

What Lilian enjoys in him is his *presence* and the mystery such a being provides as well as the comfort of what she feels to be a secure relationship—the son/mother relationship. Slowly, however, Gerard begins feeling paralyzed by Lilian's power and seeks excuses not to see her. "I have to take care of my mother," he tells Lilian. Because of her possessive nature his sleep is filled with nightmares. He begins to view Lilian not as a positive mother figure but as a vampire feeding on his blood, destroying him slowly and ruthlessly and without realizing it.

Jay, Lilian's next lover, is a bohemian and an irresponsible, mother-obsessed young man who arouses her passion. "His helplessness, made him the *homme fatal* for such a woman." He is a born dilettante and dabbles. He is a "sprite and faun, and playboy of the mother-bound world." When effort is needed in any form, such as to complete a painting, he stops work. Improvisation is his forte, discipline and travail his enemies. He acts naturally in all circumstances, relaxed, "loosely flowing, emotionally." He is Lilian's perfect mate. When there are decisions required or obligations to meet, he withers. In such circumstances Lilian is "immense" and "strong," the kind of woman who gives him solace, shelters and protects him. She is "the soundproof mother, the shockproof mother of man." She feels his maternal cravings and answers them; he is her confessor, collaborator, and lover all in one.

Jay's inability to persevere in any chosen field, his desire to live as an outcast, and his attraction to the criminal types are manifestations of his rebellious outlook. His friend Faustin, an incarnation of Jay's rational function, tells him, "You must hold on to something." But Jay rejects his advice. "I never hold on. Why hold on? Whatever you hold on to dies." Café life is delineated. It is here that Jay finds his greatest joy. He draws on the tabletops and disperses his energies most flippantly. It is this insouciance Lilian seeks. She longs to dissolve into him, to scatter her pain, and to vanish into oblivion.

Djuna is Lilian's counterpart: remote, cold, detached, introverted. "It was like a meeting of two chemicals exactly balanced, fusing and foaming with the pleasure of achieved proportions." Djuna is the thinking type: her assets are insight, evaluating power, ability to judge and experience a mental life, and to abstract and theorize. Her eyes are compared to "the inner chamber like the photographer's dark room" and give "the impression of a larger vision of the world." She quickly transforms the personal pain into a collective experience, the individual situation into the mythical. When looking out into the world, she perceives it inwardly, thereby increasing the scope of her vision.

Djuna embodies the element water, that unfathomable preformal unconscious sphere—the *fons et origo*. The primeval ocean circulates throughout her being and within her fluid domain she stores her secrets, wisdom, and arcana. Her inner world does not dissolve; on the contrary, her withdrawals, descent, and meditations allow her to discover her potential and enlarge her frame of reference.

Born in utmost poverty and reared in an orphan asylum, Djuna hungers for food and love, "the appearance of hunger" always remaining on her face. As an outlet for her feelings of emptiness and alienation, she spends much of her time dreaming. And her reveries are so realistic and powerful that frequently upon arising she feels she has "lost an entire universe of legends, myths, figures, and cities. . . ." But Djuna's inner world is dark. "Her being had received no sun, no food, no air, no warmth, no love." However, the bereavement of her early years, rather than manifesting itself in hate, transmutes into love. She is playing father, mother, cousin, friend to all those who need her.

Because she dispenses kindness and tenderness to Lilian, Djuna fulfills her satellite function. Lilian warms to her embrace and begins identifying with her. In their relationship rituals are established that resemble those practiced in primitive societies. Each revels in "presenting proofs of worship and devotion." Djuna guides Lilian, the tempestuous animal, "flaring, uncontrolled, wild, blind." In time, however, Lilian's pattern resumes: possession follows love. She thinks by giving Djuna material gifts she can own and therefore keep her. On one occasion Lilian scatters the gifts "through the room like fragments of Miro's circus painting." Lilian's relationship was one of self-destruction: she not only thought she loved Djuna, but she wanted to become her. In order to divest herself of her own identity, she began wearing Djuna's clothes, spoke and walked as she did, affected her entire demeanor. The ritual was transubstantiation: a communion of flesh and blood. Like the primitive, Lilian thought that by a religious communion she would acquire her friend's power and strength.

In all of her relationships (be it with Gerard, Jay, or Djuna), Lilian attempts to destroy herself, covertly, because she dislikes herself. Unable to accept her negative, or shadow, characteristics, she tries to hide them, since to her they are distasteful. Rather than understanding the factors at stake, she confines herself deeper in each of her loves, imprisoning and stifling her being, thus extinguishing all vestiges of life and making evolution impossible.

My escape brought me no liberation. Every night I dream the same dream of prisons and struggles to escape. It is as if only my body escaped, and not my feelings. My feelings were left over there like roots dangling when you tear a plant too violently. Violence means nothing. And it does not free one.

Lilian's feelings of self-destruction and deprecation are conveyed in her piano playing. One afternoon, giving a recital in a "golden salon," she attacks the piano as if it were her enemy, a personification of her shadow characteristics whose strength she seeks to destroy by hammering them down. "She overwhelmed it [the piano], she tormented it, crushed it. She played with all the intensity, as if the piano must be possessed or possess her." Her aggressiveness and fiery energy act as a compensatory device for what she considers her failure: her inability to achieve balance, harmony, and fulfillment.

The concert scene is detached from the rest of *Ladders to Fire*. It is depicted as a painting: the canvas, "a golden salon" where Lilian gives her concert, outside a garden with its succulent green plants and trees, and three mirrors placed in the garden that reflect and at the same time shatter the image of the performer inside. Djuna, seated in the garden, listens to the powerful tones and observes Lilian through the open doors via the reflections in the mirror—dismembered like a cubist painting, a replication of the fractured psyche.

The concert scene is an example of Nin's "space fiction." Rather than remaining on a horizontal level, the enormous motility Lilian experiences as she plays the piano is conveyed through verticality—not outward this time, but inward. The Orphic style, as defined by Apollinaire, is the art of "painting new structures out of elements which have not been borrowed from the visual sphere, but have been created entirely by the artist himself, and been endowed by him with fullness and reality."[8] In Nin's piano scene the mirror reflections that cast variegated light/shadow rays alter contours throughout the interlude. The play of lights causes a dramatic interchange between subject and object; the verdant trees and plants in the garden, the hammered tonalities of the piano, and the artist within the golden salon heighten and slacken the tensions involved. Lilian emerges as an earthbound creature, a part of nature's world.

"Bread and the Wafer" suggests even more strongly Lilian's self-destructive attitude. Still without identity and unable to accept traits she considers negative, Lilian is endlessly pursuing her goalless existence in attempts to merge with whatever male or female she admires at the moment. Like the churchgoer who celebrates communion to divest himself of his mortal self, so Lilian aims to enter her deity's world and being.

Lilian's friend Sabina is like the Sabine women of old, who were abducted by the descendents of Romulus for reproductive purposes so that their state would thrive. Powerful, independent, energetic, and explosive, "Only Sabina's ladder led to fire." A fire principle, Sabina is passionate and restless. Her exterior, "dressed in red and silver, the searing red and silver siren cutting a pathway through her flesh," reflects an inner energy. The first time she looks at Sabina, Lilian has the feeling that "Everything will burn!" However, Sabina's fiery nature could be destructive; she feels little and her predatory nature allows her to live for the moment, without guilt, fear, or love. Sabina is the only protagonist in *Ladders to Fire* to succeed in life, to rise in the hierarchy of beings and values.

As a solar force, she is the guiding principle, the flame in Lilian's life. No one can escape her if he falls within her grasp. Sabina is spiritual energy (libido) personified: that factor alchemists considered capable of regenerating life. She can also sear and burn, cut relationships, prevent growth, and bring about death and destruction.

A sensation type, Sabina adapts easily to reality. She can relate to people because she knows how to handle them and extract from them what is of import to her. She is sophisticated, a *femme fatale*, a siren: the song she sings is always sweet and enriching. Men and women alike may be attracted to her lair, where she will devour them. When Jay first meets her he dislikes her. He feels unconsciously her claws about his neck; later she becomes his mistress. Lilian too is caught in her web; their liaison, however, is disappointing. What Sabina feeds on is power. She will arouse but not fulfill; beguile and then discard; ensnare and drag her victim down. Lilian "saw Sabina's eyes burning, heard her voice so rusty and immediately felt drowned in her beauty."

Sabina is rootless and unfettered; she is unburdened with self-doubt, self-hate, or guilt. She tells her life story to Lilian "swiftly, like the accelerated scenes of a boken machine," mentioning her love affairs, parties, flagellations, drug addiction, encounters with the police. Sabina "beck-oned and lured one into her world, and then blurred the passageways, confused the images and ran away in fear of detection." Sabina is Jay's female counterpart, not to be trusted, natural, free, fervent.

There are two Sabinas: the outer woman and the inner hidden being. Wherever she goes, Sabina seeks to maintain an image, her collective mask—that of the thoughtful, kind, faithful friend. But her world consists of a series of pre-tenses, adornments, costumes, gold, and glitter, and she is constantly playing the role of seductress. Lilian is her prey. "I destroy people without meaning to," Sabina confesses. And Lilian emerges with Sabina, longing to be her, in a psychic suicide.

One of the most arresting images in *Ladders to Fire* is the description of the party Jay and Lilian give at their Montparnasse studio, which concludes the novel. At this party all the characters in *Ladders to Fire* come together. The floor of the studio is squared off like a chessboard. Jay is the Chess Player who moves about the squares singling out each of the guests for a satiric, angry, or loving inter-change. No one knows the meaning of Jay's game. "He was content with the displacements and did not share in the developments. He would then stand in the corner of the room again and survey the movements with a semitone smile." Djuna, the woman of many moods, is introduced to an architect who has created a world of intimate relation-ships through a house of mysteries, spiral staircases and secret rooms—corresponding to Djuna's inner world: her "night face, her shadows and her darkness." Strong and unfettered like Jay, Sabina is not moved and does not fear his attempt to ridicule her. "She merely turned her face away." Then she walks proudly among the guests, dem-onstrating her power over them. Whereas Djuna lives in "the cities of the interior," Sabina has no permanent abode. "She was always arriving and leaving undetected, as through a series of trap doors." But the guests feel remote and alienated from the world about them and from themselves. It is "the least attended party in literature," Nin wrote. "No one was there. They were all absent."[9] Nin described her literary technique with regard to the Chess-Player Party.

I wanted to bring all the characters together in some sort of symbolic game. . . . I was describing now how people were at a party but how, when obsessed by other preoccupations, they were present on the surface but absent emotionally, psychologically *not* there. By symbolism I made the party transparent so you could see the inner drama as you might trace a fracture under an X ray.[10]

The entire chessboard and Chess Player sequence had been inspired by one of Martha Graham's dances, stylized and archetypal in its ramifications. Each character is placed on the stage to impose his or her power and presence upon the others; lighting, gesture, form, the general rhythmic undulations gather the disparate protagonists into a new unity. The scene is not depicted for its representational value but for its emotional effect. Nin's protagonists are isolated on an imaginary stage, each moving about on squares arranged to create tension, excitement, expectancy, and drama. Djuna, Sabina, and Stella glide here and there in trancelike spontaneity, depending, it seems, on some mysterious inner faculty to arouse one or another person. The painter de Chirico once said, "The whole nostalgia of the infinite is revealed to us behind the geometrical precision of the square."[11] A whole universe is present in the unforgettable movements of Stella, Sabina, and Djuna as they make their way through the Montparnasse studio, each stepping with or against Jay's rhythmic advances and departures.

At the party's conclusion, Lilian, in a frenzy of self-doubt, is left alone on one of the squares "to commit her daily act of self-destruction." Ashamed of everything about herself, she deprecates her dress, jewels, hair, conversation, even her silences. Nothing remains.

A complete house-wrecking service. Every word, smile, act, silver jewel, lying on the floor, with the emerald green dress, and even Djuna's image of Lilian to which she had often turned for comfort that too lay shattered on the ground. Nothing to salvage. A mere pile of flaws. A little pile of ashes from the bonfire of self-criticism.

The Chess Player saw a woman crumbling down on a couch as if her inner frame had collapsed, smiled at her drunkenness and took no notice of the internal suicide.

Lilian's psychic suicide at the finale is the only fitting conclusion for *Ladders to Fire*. By divesting herself of her personality through Sabina and Djuna, she became a void, a maw—and felt her emptiness. Each of the women—the men too—who entered her life as dormant aspects of her personality, cut her off still further from her roots; each pursued the depersonalization process, scattering the fragments of her being hither and yon until she was no more.

Children of the Albatross

Children of the Albatross is divided into two parts: "The Sealed Room" and "The Café." Both parts deal with the private world of childhood and its arcane rituals and innocent cruelties. Two worlds, that of children and that of the albatross, help define the theme and the atmosphere. Children imply growth and futurity; the albatross exemplifies a "glowing" force, a "phosphorescence" that comes from the magic world of childhood, which Nin describes as both irresponsible and responsible; it is a period when young people express their joys as well as their feelings of timidity and fear.

"The Sealed Room" focuses on Djuna. We learn through flashback that she is a professional dancer. No longer poor, she has discovered "the air, space, and lightness of her own nature." In a series of exquisite sequences, where language takes on the configurations of arabesques, Djuna's inner climate is transmuted into linear and spatial contours. Michael, Djuna's lover and mirror image, enters "her blue and white climate." Reminiscent of a Botticelli painting, his walk is "like a dance in which his gentleness of step carried him through air, space, and silence." Donald becomes Michael's lover. He is vengeful, quixotic, and egotistical. Paul, a tender seventeen, lives with Djuna in the "sealed room." He cannot face reality. Together they listen to César Franck's *Symphony in D Minor* and experience the emotional patterns of the music as their own; they fuse amid the pulsating rhythms ("exaltation, dissolution" of feelings). In a moment of self-analysis Djuna wonders whether she is fated to be attracted forever to those "airy young men who love in a realm like the realm of the birds."

"The Café" takes us into the adventurous world of Sabina, Lilian, and Djuna. They have not changed. Sabina is still the *femme fatale;* her secretary is her *raison d'être.* She refuses to give anyone her address and enjoys donning personae and changing her name as frequently as she does her lovers. For her, men are a game. None of her many liaisons, however, has brought her satisfaction. Lilian is still the powerful, earthy but insecure woman of *Ladders to Fire.* She is still in love with Jay, incessantly trying to possess and enclose him within her being. On one occasion, she puts on Sabina's cape (her persona) and forces herself to have a liaison with a stranger in a hotel room—to be like Sabina. But unlike her friend, she feels no sensations of joy or independence. Jay is drawn to Djuna, although Sabina is the only one he wants to paint. But he finds Djuna's company relaxing and wants her to remain with them because only she gives him feelings of well-being.

Children of the Albatross as a whole is comparable to a theatrical spectacle. The house, which is the most important image in the book, is the decor. The dance, the vehicle used by Nin to express the protagonists' feelings and inner climate, becomes the catalyst; it arouses tension and weaves its detours and contours around the proceedings. The space into which the configurations, both amorphous and concrete, are incised, becomes an active and compelling force in the drama.

We are told that Djuna lives in an old house with a garden in the outskirts of Paris. Removed from the crowd, she inhabits a world of her own. Djuna's house is her kingdom. Within this house shines an inner light that becomes visible at night; and when illuminated, the house stands resplendent and aflame in the solitude of its surroundings. An awesome and solemn world is conjured up here, reminiscent of those ancient mysteries practiced in hidden sanctuaries and remote forested areas. Djuna's house is personal and impersonal: "It was the house of the myth." Each room and each window mirrors a variety of tonalities, moods, color combinations; each fuses into one visual image, reflecting and deflecting levels of consciousness. The house is not *one* domain, but *all* domains. It encloses the disparate facets of the protagonists' inner world. It takes on the collective power of a house of worship with its treasures, magic, and divinities. "It was the ritual they sensed, tasted, smelled. Too different from the taste and smell of their own houses. It took them out of the present. They took on an air of temporary guests."

Not only is the location of the house important, but even more significant is that Djuna's house has twelve windows of which there is "one shuttered window" that does not lead to any room. In contrast to the "multiple tongues," argumentations and contradictions that emanate from the other windows, this *black* window, this one unknown factor, generates fear and terror.

Djuna has chosen the house because she knows she needs roots and solidity as well as airiness. The house gives her that solidity; the windows, the airiness: outward vision and inner contemplation. Nin compares the tree in Djuna's garden to the house, dual also in its visual implications. The tree is deeply implanted in the earth whereas its branches look toward freedom and spirituality in the limitless expanse above.

. . . it seemed to have sprouted out of the earth like a tree, so deeply grooved it was within the old garden. It had no cellar and the rooms rested right on the ground. Below the rugs, she felt, was the earth. One could take root here, feel at one with the house and garden, take nourishment from them like the plants.

The shuttered window has to be investigated. That area as it is represents an impasse; it also spells mystery and excitement. One day, Djuna reasons, she may find the path and entrance leading to the hidden room, its contours, its meaning. In ancient days, rooms played important roles in initiation rituals. For the initiate, the real room is the inner sanctuary; the exterior domain is merely the façade. Acolytes experienced the "death" of their profane self and the "birth" of the new spiritual being in these remote chambers. The object of initiation was to lead into illumination: to experience the transcendental light, or center, of Self. Djuna's secret room, which represents her inner being, has to be investigated, its contents brought to light, and its treasures understood. Therefore the path leading to the room must be found so that what remains within its folds can be nurtured and allowed to live freely, no more repressed and rejected and smoldering in darkness. Whenever she is able to shed the world of perpetual blackness and to achieve a modicum of clarity of mind and spirit, Djuna hopes to experience independence and fulfillment as distinguished from potentiality.

Djuna's unformed and unrealized thoughts, sensations, and feelings are contained within this "sealed room." Like hierophants they are endowed with divine power, possess a magic of their own, but cannot function properly or to her advantage because they are incarcerated in her closeted inner world. Each time they emerge, they limp along, float about, but never really achieve solid footing, never bring her fulfillment.

The twelve windows are significant because, like the twelve signs of the zodiac or the twelve months of the year, they represent a cyclical spatio-temporal domain that incorporates the four elements (earth, water, fire, air) and the three alchemical principles (sulfur, salt, mercury). The forces that cause life and growth are present; the objects are solid; but the structure is inadequate. No symphonic tone poem can be composed until a unity of personality comes into being.

When Djuna looks out into the world from her window, she is at the same time looking within. Her face is reflected in the glass: thus, a two-way dynamism takes place. As she peers into her inner cosmos where linear time is no longer a factor, she experiences her past as though it were a present reality. She is in her orphanage, the solitary child, a product of a dreary and poverty-stricken existence. Suddenly, she sees a young man passing beneath the orphanage window and falls in love with him. The light from the outside world, its activity and excitement, has nourished her inner scape and activates it. So the past arouses her present sensations and vision. Yet, the glass that separates her from her friends also causes her to feel alienated and solitary. She observes more closely the windowpane and her reflection in it; she studies her facial contours and the expression in her eyes. Djuna objectifies and, in so doing, begins to define her acts and to will her destiny. "Henceforth she possessed this power: whatever emotion would ravish or torment her, she could bring it before a mirror, look at it, and separate herself from it. And she thought she had found a way to master sorrow." Unlike Narcissus, she does not drown in her image. Her ego is not going to be dispersed and then eclipsed; on the contrary, she uses the mirror image to build and structure her future.

Nin's use of the vocabulary and iconography of the dance

—its stylized gestures, rhythms, tonalities, and beats—to delineate her protagonists, both physically and emotionally, adds another dimension to *Children of the Albatross*. Djuna's painful years in the orphanage, for example, are compared to "walking on crutches"; happier times have changed her "overnight into a dance in which she discovered the air, space and lightness of her own nature." It is the dance that has endowed Djuna with the earth power to emerge from the orphanage, out of poverty, out of an unregenerate past. "The flow of images set to music had descended from her head to her feet and she ceased to feel as one who had been split into two pieces by some great invisible saber cut." When dejected, Djuna's feelings manifest themselves in halting pirouettes, in broken beats, not in measured movements. "*I am the dancer who falls*, always, into traps of depression, breaking my heart and my body almost at every turn, losing my tempo and my lightness." Djuna sways with her body and taps with her feet, recording the minutest nuances in structured mimetic action. "The dance gained in perfection, a perfection born of an accord between their gestures; born of her submission and his domination."

Nin evoked the marvelous legatos or quick leaps into the air of Michel Fokine, Léonide Massine, or Anna Pavlova, when she sought to express the immateriality of Djuna's soul: "The body recovered, the body dancing (hadn't she been the woman in quest of her body once lost by a shattering blow—submerged, and now floating again on the surface where uncrippled human beings lived in a world of pleasure like the Fair?)"

Nin choreographs Djuna's inner wanderings in a series of sculptured frescoes that often resemble Ida Rubinstein's unforgettable incarnation of Cleopatra set against a Bakst décor of lapis lazuli and orange. The parallel is particularly apt during Djuna's moments of elation when she attempts to lure her bait into her fold. When experiencing an inner exoticism, Djuna's gestures, walk, and contours bring to mind Rimski-Korsakov's *Scheherazade,* with its sumptuous rhythms and orchestrations and the sensuality of blues, sapphires, and greens. Djuna's partner, Michael, becomes a voluptuous young animal who dances around his queen, always pirouetting within her shadow. Nostalgia enters as Djuna watches a merry-go-round: "It turned and her feelings with it." She realizes at this juncture that something within her has broken; she no longer can dance or even live as others do. She is different. She needs her house, but she also needs to feast on the outside world—on young, vibrant beings. She needs to look out through the windows of her home and reach out through the dance that eases her entree into life.

Djuna, Lilian, Sabina, Paul, Michael, and Donald resemble Balinese dancers—actors in a sacred ceremony. Their gestures are transforming agents transcending the domain of appearances and revealing their mysterious inner worlds. Their hidden intentions cannot be dissimulated any more; they become visible on the stage Nin created. Perceived at times in the form of an elevated arm, a lowered finger, an arched leg, a glance, or a walk, each protagonist is endowed with magical force, empowered to transform the amorphous feeling into its concrete realization.

The image of Djuna walking through snow replicates the iciness she feels.

Walking through the snow, carrying her muff like an obsolete wand no longer possessed of the power to create the personage she needed, she felt herslf walking through a desert of snow.

Her body muffled in furs, her heart muffled like her steps, and the pain of living muffled as by the deepest rich carpets, while the thread of Ariadne which led everywhere, right and left, like scattered footsteps in the snow, tugged and pulled within her memory and she began to pull upon this thread (silk for the days of marvel and cotton for the bread of everyday living which was always a little stale) as one pulls upon a spool, and she heard the empty wooden spool knock against the floor of different houses.

Djuna's walk reaches metaphysical proportions through an alliance between earth and heaven that is now encapsulated in her being. As in Balinese theater, space is not empty; it is full, active, and alive.

Michael's walk, in another scene, is reminiscent of Siva's Tandava dance and arouses ethereal forces with each breath he takes.

It was a walk like a dance in which the gentleness of the steps carried him through air, space and silence in a sentient minuet in accord with his partner's mood, his leaf-green eyes obeying every rhythm, attentive to harmony, fearful of discord, with an excessive care for the other's intent.

Action is wedded to space; it generates rhythms, enhances analogies, and inflates form and feeling.

For the first time, as she danced away from him, encircled by young men's arms, he measured the great space they had been swimming through, measured it exactly as others measure the distance between planets.

The mileage of space he had put between himself and Djuna. The lighthouse of the eyes alone could traverse such immensity!

And now, after such elaborations in space, so many figures interposed between them, the white face of Iseult, the burning face of Catherine, all of which he had interpreted as mere elaborations of his enjoyment of her, now suddenly appeared not as ornaments but as obstructions to his possession of her.

Sounds, gestures, rhythms, and colors encroach upon Djuna's sense of freedom and dilute the airy feeling she previously has experienced, if only for a moment. Michael's shadow, like Redon's divine eye, intrudes and stifles her.

He absorbed her dark, long, swinging hair, the blue eyes never at rest, a little slanted, quick to close their curtains too, quick to laugh, but more often thirsty, absorbing like a mirror. She swallowed the pupil to receive these images of others but one felt they did not vanish altogether as they would on a mirror: one felt a thirsty being absorbing reflections and drinking words and faces, into herself for a deep communion with them.

Djuna's personality was envisaged as a dance in space. Nin went "beyond form to achieve poetry." Like Miró in his canvas *The Hunter*, Nin took a group of objects, reduced them in size, and placed them within a circle. In such a context they not only generate a sense of mystery, but are reminiscent of archetypal constructs, forms that gain in significance throughout the work.[12] In the description of Djuna's house, poetry emanates from the configurations of the objects as well as from their disposition: form and feeling inflate, rhythms accelerate.

Nin created her own bestiary with its motifs, fantastic appearances, biomorphic forms, and insolent shapes. Each motif enlarges the reader's way of seeing the characters and experiencing the emotions involved. Man and animal are one; animate and inanimate are fused into a single cosmic force. Michael's feminine personality, for example, his chatter and perpetual undulations are compared to a bird's head as it turns about like a weather vane: ". . . the little dance of alertness, the petulance of the mouth pursed for a small kiss . . . the flutter and perk of prize birds, all adornment and chance."

"The Sealed Room" concludes on a musical note. As Djuna and Paul listen to César Franck's *Symphony in D Minor*, with its mystic overtones and its idealism, the protagonists' emotions seem to take on breadth and power. Franck's emphasis on theme, exposition, tone, timber, and serial pattern is an expression of the eternal quality of human pain, as well as joy. For Djuna and Paul, feeling is uppermost at this point, as the music dictates: "In César Franck's symphony there was immediate exaltation, dissolution in feeling. . . . Over and over again in this musical ascension of emotion, the stairway of fever was climbed and deserted before one reached explosion."

It is through Franck's symphony that Djuna begins to understand her emotions as these are replicated in harmonies, polyphonies, and the structured order of the musical phrases. She now understands the link (as mystics of old

had, such as Pythagoras who believed in the interrelatedness
of sound, meter, and number with the planetary spheres)
between herself and those attracted to her fold, as well as
between herself and the world at large. Music symbolizes an
intermediate zone between the material and the undifferentiated realm.[13] Music expresses the fluidity of her feelings
and generates love; its "obsessional return to minor themes,"
creates an "endless tranquility" within her. Like a com-
panion, music helps Djuna through her ordeal, "bringing
messages of softness and trust."

"The Café" introduces readers to another world. The
sealed room with its exciting mysteries is gone; we are now
led into the conventional world, with its routines as well as
its exotic cast. Because coffeehouses were gathering places
for gossip, gambling, and the like, they aroused and har-
bored fantasy worlds and brought distant lands of enchantment within the drinker's reach. Many artists and writers—
among them Gauguin, Manet, Baudelaire, Verlaine—have
haunted cafés, where they enjoyed the conviviality of friendships and allowed their imaginations to haunt an archaic
past.

It is in the café that Nin's protagonists meet and radiate
outward. Here they are forced into an unlimited spatial area
where infinite perspectives increase illusion, but, in so doing,
also imbricate feelings of malaise into the atmosphere. Limitless perspectives bring on a sense of disorientation and loss
of identity. An abyss is created; a void grows as each protagonist finds himself floundering about.[14]

In an unlimited spatial area the reader is kept from
identifying with the space directly before him. He is not part
of it, nor does he feel linked to the object he views. What he
observes therefore is no longer an extension of his own
being. He feels himself suspended in space, in a nongravita-
tional universe. Such an atmosphere is generated in a superb
image of Djuna as she awakens from a dream so deeply felt

that, when opening her eyes, she wants to push "aside the heavy shroud of veils, a thousand layers of veils and with a sensation similar to that of the trapezist who has been swinging in vast spaces, and suddenly feels again in his two hands the coarse touch of the swinging cord." A primeval past converges on the café. Distant lands swing across the visual screen; kinetic ideograms dart forth, cruelly, impeccably. Djuna feels these parallel forces within her like veils of guilt, remorse, anger, and pain. She tears at them and rejects them. Yet they remain implacable, like forebodings tyrannizing her.

Lilian carries a similar dream within her. She considers herself a pawn, an object reduced to powerlessness, an element cut off from the landscape, a supplemental form. She yearns for a fantasy life that would bring her solace and for the dream that would yield her "ultimate knowledge." Yet, she knows that it is in the world at large—in life—that she may "be rescued from anonymity and oblivion." A creature torn between love and the fear of rejection, she views her situation as catastrophic. She experiences only sorrow; but the greater her feelings of rejection, the more aggressive and possessive she becomes. "I want the world to be all mine." When she finally understands Jay's fascination for Sabina and Djuna, excessively tormented, she goes into her bedroom and escapes in her piano playing. The fervency of her feelings are sounded in clusters of tones.

The image of the café opened the second part of *Children of the Albatross;* the streets conclude it. The encounters centering about the café have encouraged the protagonists to seek their paths through a sequence of daring harmonic progressions. Djuna, Sabina, and Lilian frequently find themselves caught in a maze of crooked and winding streets of currents and crosscurrents of emotion that pull them about, cut and bruise them. Yet, they pursue their course of deepening self-awareness. Although still lacking a central key feeling they try, each in her own way, to build a world for themselves following an unerring straight line. No longer atonal beings with atomized personalities, their worlds have taken on a semblance of unity.

Four-Chambered Heart

Four-Chambered Heart is the most poignant of the novels comprising *Cities of the Interior*. It focuses on Djuna, whose passivity and blindness with regard to her motivations lead to a virtual dispersion of her ego. The metaphor of the novel's title comes from a medical book that defines the heart "as an organ . . . consisting of four chambers. . . . A wall separates the chambers on the left side from those on the right and no direct communication is possible between them."

Djuna rents a houseboat on the Seine and here lives out her passionate encounter with Rango, a Guatemalan guitar player. Their relationship neither grows nor evolves; it experiences a condition of stasis comparable to the houseboat that vegetates in its moorings, never budging, and that Rango never repairs. Djuna's and Rango's lives are like "deserts where vultures perpetuated their encirclement." Death, not life, emerges.

Zora, Rango's wife, is described as a "professional beggar." She is ill and uses her sickness as a tool to dominate her passive and dependent husband. Djuna becomes ensnared in the destructive dialogues between husband and wife. Feeling pity for Zora, she brings her clothes and furs that the sick woman stores for safekeeping in a trunk. Rango joins the Communist Party, and Zora is convinced Djuna encouraged him to do so to force him out of Zora's life. In a fit of anger she comes onto the houseboat and with a long hat pin tries to stab Djuna. Only after this incident does Djuna begin to understand her inertia and her own faceless nature.

The haunting and insalubrious quality implicit in *Four-Chambered Heart* is reminiscent of Carson McCullers's first novel, *The Heart Is a Lonely Hunter* (1940), which focuses on two mutes and the isolation they experience in life. Rather than two mutes, Nin features three psychologically blind protagonists—parasites that feed on one another and are unable to perceive the other's foibles. Both works may be looked upon as parables of man's spiritual isolation; his need for communication and his escape in love that is but illusion.[15]

The image of the houseboat expresses to perfection the protagonists' painful solitude and their need to find some semblance of happiness in dream relationships. When Djuna rented the houseboat on the Seine, she learned it had once been used as a theater for strolling players. She realizes that her life too is ephemeral, as transient as a stage play but also as exciting. To live life fully and intensely as one does during a theatrical performance is part of her hedonistic view.

The houseboat is a perfect vehicle for what Djuna looks upon as her love for Rango. Cut off from the city and from land, poised on constantly shifting waters, the houseboat represents her inability to accept terra firma, that is, the stability of conventional relationships. The swaying of the houseboat, reacting perpetually to the undulating waters, lulls her into a state of peace and tranquillity, that preformal world where the unconscious holds full sway. "We want to find an island, a solitary cell, where we can dream in peace together." Ambivalence also marks Djuna's life on the houseboat: the need for constant motion and an inability to "break away from [the] moorings, to go on a long voyage." The houseboat and her relationship with Rango give her protection and security, but they lead to an impasse.

Water is the most important image in *Four-Chambered Heart*. It is on water that Djuna and Rango fix their visions, mold their love, experience their anger. As mentioned in an earlier chapter, the principle of all things resides in water. Liquid, as opposed to solid, insinuates itself everywhere, circulates throughout nature and makes for growth, fertility, and greenness. Thus it stands for virtuality and change, perpetual motion. Water is a transitional element, a mediator between life and death—between the poet and his creation. In too great quantity, however, water may lead to decay, mold, fungi, and drowning. Under certain circumstances flooding ensues. If Djuna had been aware of the parasitic existence she was living, she could have changed matters and perhaps a creative relationship could have resulted.

The windowed house of *Children of the Albatross*, with its mysterious sealed room, is gone. Djuna is singing her lyrical prose stanzas on water, out in the open for all to hear. But like the house, the boat becomes a symbol of containment, a microcosm where the space-time continuum plays a dominant role between the lovers.

From the houseboat emerges the dream, irreality, illusion—and disillusion. "We're navigating," Rango says; but he is fostering a lie. He rejects the outside world and builds his own castles in eternity. Brawn and all instinct, Rango is a primitive with an anthropoid psyche. The power of his music (symbolically feeling) hypnotizes and captivates Djuna as it had countless other women. Unable to understand the workaday world, he can neither provide for his wife nor for Djuna; nor can he repair the boat when it springs a leak. He vegetates and thrives on love, pursuing the physical life and accepting the comfort Djuna offers him so fully.

Obstacles intrude upon what Rango and Djuna would like to think of as an idyllic existence. He becomes jealous of Djuna's past loves. His jealousy reaches such a peak that "His face would darken with anger, and he made violent gestures." Words catapult forth and passion inundates his being. Jay, Paul, and the others seem to live again at this moment; they become actual presences that participate in events. For weeks on end, the past is integrated into the present, more powerful as memories than it had ever been in real life. Jay and Paul occupy Rango's and Djuna's thoughts, dominate their relationship, destroy their world of dreams that Djuna has so carefully nurtured in the houseboat. "You are the one constantly reminding me of his existence," she tells Rango. His jealousy, resulting from his fear of losing her, could easily shatter their love. "But more dangerous was the death of love for lack of replenishment." Love does not vanish from "illness and wounds, it dies of weariness, of withering, of tarnishings." To be pitied is "the lover who murders love," and Rango kills their love.

The Jays and Pauls of bygone years are cut off from Djuna's present life; they are fragments without significance, like abandoned stones in the middle of a street. It is Rango who gives them significance and import by resurrecting them. Djuna's past love experiences are like "immobilized instants" that nourish themselves and breathe fresh life in new contexts. That Djuna's past lovers are meaningless to her at this time is relatively unimportant in her relationship with Rango. Their *presences* dominate her life; they have become something so potent as to nearly destroy her happiness. They seem like mysterious divinities emerging from some remote world and, as Michel Butor phrased it, take on new levels of meaning and enter profounder spheres of the psyche.[16] Jay and Paul refuse to vanish because Rango will not allow it. "Your jealousy is necrophilic!" Djuna states. "You're opening tombs!" She accuses him of killing their love and of driving these forgotten men "into another chamber of her heart, an isolated chamber without communicating passage into the one inhabited by Rango." Isolation, rather than diminishing, grows more acute.

Rango's anger reaches holocaust force. He burns the books Djuna had read at the time of her former liaisons, the books she had discussed and enjoyed with her lovers. Djuna does not stop him from his destructive acts, instead she aids him. Fire, like passion, heaves its searing flames and encapsulates everything: words, books, feelings—all is submerged in chaos.

Djuna, however, is not burning her past. She is burning books she does not like, to which she cannot relate, works of social novelists of the 1920s and 1930s whose naturalistic style is anathema to her: Theodore Dreiser, John Dos Passos, John Steinbeck, James T. Farrell. Their crude descriptions of society and their air of social commitment seem hollow to her; their characters' perpetually hopeless lives offend her sensibilities. Their lack of poetry depresses her. She views American novels with the same feelings of revulsion that she has toward Chaim Soutine's paintings with their chunks of carved carcasses or plucked fowl. Djuna relentlessly searches for illusion, not for dismemberment, and for beauty, not for sordid play. Djuna expresses her anger toward these novelists because she believes them to be inauthentic. They lived their narratives intellectually not viscerally.

Words words words and no revelation of the pitfalls, the abysms in which human beings found themselves . . . Novels promising experience, and then remaining on the periphery, opening no wells, preparing no one for the crises, the pitfalls, the wars, and the traps of human life. Teaching nothing, revealing nothing, cheating us of truth, of immediacy, of reality.

Zora is perhaps the most interesting character in *Four-Chambered Heart*. Nin studied in her the personality of the hypochondriac. Zora's illness serves her needs; it was created in order to dominate and to hold onto Rango. Zora considers herself—and Rango can only agree—completely helpless. She cannot cook, clean, or fend for herself in any way. Rango does everything for her, and when away from her, he feels corroded by guilt. He blames himself for her condition: his infidelities have led to her many problems, which range from heart to throat conditions. And Zora in her own subtle way corroborates Rango's feelings.

At first Djuna questions the validity of Rango's attitude: "She was not your wife, she was your sick child, long before I came." Rango asks Djuna to help care for her: "She is very ill and you might help her." The masochistic circle is complete when Djuna, also weakly structured, feels pity for Zora. She too is blinded by the master artificer that Zora has become. Zora's techniques to elicit compassion, tears, and sorrow are extraordinary. Djuna succumbs to Zora's flattery; Zora knows how to play on Djuna's kindness: "I knew sooner or later he would love another woman, and I am glad it's you because you are kind, and you will not take him away from me. I need him." Djuna, always compassionate, leaps at the prospect of being able to help a sick woman. Not once does she realize that Zora's illness is not grave and that her inability to see the situation allows this unhealthy dynamic to pursue its destructive course.

Zora not only dominates the round but, like a circus trainer, she also orders the rhythmic pace of the proceedings. At the beginning of their love affair, Rango spends every night with Djuna on the houseboat. As Zora's symptoms grow progressively worse, he spends only two nights a week with Djuna, then only one. The conflict between the two women grows concomitantly more powerful, each vying for the same man. And Rango, the pawn, exists between two destructive forces. The love affair slackens in pace as Rango spends more time with his wife. By the same token, the more passive and submissive Djuna becomes, the greater is her victimization by Zora. She finds herself falling into the Rango pattern, rather than creating her own way.

Rango and Zora may be looked upon as facets of Djuna's personality, each in conflict with the other, each attempting to relate to the other. Clothed in isolation, each veers into its lonely "chamber." It is not just by chance that Djuna's multiple selves are compared to Marcel Duchamp's *Nude Descending a Staircase*: just as the motif of that canvas is not chaotic but systematized and regulated, so Djuna's love sequence with Rango also appears, at least peripherally, as an integrated whole. Actually, it is fragmented and reconstructed in various forms and textured tones: an atomized self replicated in triangles, cones, and spheres. Djuna's cut-up psyche is mangled and shattered.

That aspect of Djuna as projected onto Zora is her weak, frail, limp self which, through sickness, elicits pity from her victims and thus gains a stranglehold over them. Zora feeds on sickness. From the library she has taken out books on illnesses and relates the symptoms she reads about to herself: "I've marked all the pages which apply to me. Just look at all these markings. Sometimes I think I have all the sicknesses one can have!"

There is another part of Djuna, however, that is revolted by the woman whose power is so great, whose psyche is so sick. The anger is not aimed at Zora, rather it is resentment aimed at her own inner being. Djuna is that weak, sick woman in projection, who allows herself to be moved and dominated by this creature. Although she expresses devotion and compassion in all of her actions toward Zora, inwardly Djuna despises her. She hates what Zora represents within herself: that negative destructive force that turns Djuna's life into a veil of tears.

Djuna despises Zora for leading a "useless" life. Yet, here again, what she is angry about is that aspect of Zora that exists within herself. Djuna knows she is too weak to break off with Rango, too passive to assume an independent stand. Djuna/Zora is guilty of "grasping food, devotion, service, and giving absolutely nothing, less than nothing. A useless life, exhuding poison, envy, a strangling tyranny." It is no wonder that Djuna always falls in love with weak men; they are passive beings who complement her own being. There is a need within her for domination, for possession, and for security.

Djuna/Zora are distortions of a composite picture. What Duchamp said about *Nude Descending a Staircase* is applicable to Nin's creatures in *Four-Chambered Heart*: they are not beings but "an organization of kinetic elements, an expression of time and space through the abstract presentation of motion. . . ."[17] Djuna's disparate selves, with their autonomous feeling/sensations, live their lives on a stage as fragmented parts of a whole viewed throughout the novel in a perpetually differing manner according to new relationships and fresh incidents.

A *deus ex machina* brings about a break-up of the impasse between Djuna, Rango, and Zora and allows new perceptions to come into being. Rango joins the Communist Party and seeks to overthrow the Guatemalan government. Zora believes that Djuna urged him on and accuses her of taking him away from her. Djuna, always apolitical, forever uncommitted, denies such accusations. Nevertheless, in a state of insane fury, Zora rushes to the houseboat and attempts to stab Djuna with a hat pin but succeeds only in grazing her skin. The incident, however, so traumatizes Djuna that it brings her insight. The new perception comes as she is observing the continuously undulating Seine. The lulling rhythms no longer encourage a state of passivity, but rather allow her to peer more profoundly into her inner world and the disparate parts of her psyche seem to merge into a new unity. "Below the level of identity lay an ocean, an ocean of which human beings carry only a drop in their veins; but some sink below cognizance and the drop becomes a huge wave, the tide of memory, the undertows of sensation. . . ."

Djuna understands now that Zora and Rango are cast-off parts of herself, that she related to them, unconsciously, in a strange and absorbing fashion. Within Djuna there resides a mystery, an ambiguity by which each facet of her personality is drawn to another, belongs to another, yet is cut off from the other; each possesses its own void. Though Djuna seemed near to Zora and to Rango, distances exist between them. Each is *absent* to the other; each lives in his or her own closeted realm. Therefore, events are experienced on various levels throughout *Four-Chambered Heart*: consciously and unconsciously. When her vision became blurred, as though experiencing a kind of atonality within her being, she grew detached, impersonal. Her attitudes seemed discontinuous, like the music of Webern, athematic, yet controlled by the whole.

At the conclusion of *Four-Chambered Heart*, Djuna is no more the hypersensitive childlike creature of the opening. Her illusions have vanished. She understands the game of life, the play that must be part of it, the chance factor that determines the destiny of individuals. When, at the end, she walks on the quay with Rango, she sees a doll floating in the Seine. It "had committed suicide during the night." It is Djuna's childlike nature that has been cast overboard. The end of an adventure. Another round of self-interrogation and growth has begun.

Unlike Balzac's characters who are whole either in their miserliness or in their paternal obsessions, or Dostoyevsky's creatures who are always at odds with themselves, or Proust's beings who reveal their inner climate through images and interior monologues, the characters of *Four-Chambered Heart* are disparate facets of a personality, sliced and sheared for the story line, each an autonomous fragment playing out its own pulsions and repulsions on the houseboat stage, with Paris as the backdrop and the Seine as the catalyst, lulling, propelling, cradling the illusory world on its course—until it shatters like crushed glass.

A Spy in the House of Love

Unlike the previous novels comprising *Cities of the Interior*, which take place in Paris, *A Spy in the House of Love* is situated in New York. A change of scene reflects a concomitant alteration of emphasis and tone. Not anymore immersed in the youthful and romantic atmosphere of France, Nin's protagonists express their ironies and discontents in what is looked upon as an American puritanical background. Also stylistically Nin altered her course. She adopted to a great extent the New Novelists' technique: an attempt at further depersonalization of the main character; greater emphasis on cyclical time, thus delimiting the protagonist's vision and actions; repetitions of entire scenes, each time played out in a slightly different manner, thus heightening the ambiguity and multifaceted nature of life in general. The New Novelists' technique enabled Nin to present her heroine from a variety of viewpoints and in polyvalent clusters of incidents.

A Spy in the House of Love focuses on Sabina, an actress now, who thirsts for stability and continuity within her own personality (the "One and not the Multiple selves") and permanence in her relationship with men instead of the simultaneous and reckless liaisons she has known. Although she tries to confess her infidelities to her husband, to cleanse her conscience and start a new relationship with him, she fails to do so for fear of hurting him. In flashbacks the reader lives through her *amorati* with an opera singer in Provincetown and with Mambo, a *café au lait* jazz musician. But no man can fulfill her needs. The conflict within her personality becomes so acute that it gives birth to a fantasy image that takes on reality: the Lie Detector, a kind of superego or father figure, which tells her, "You wouldn't have called me if you were innocent. Guilt is the one burden human beings can't bear alone." The Lie Detector follows her everywhere like the Greek Fates. It compels her to examine her feelings with increased detachment. She does so and in this sense feels like "a spy in the house of love."

The New Novelists in France (Nathalie Sarraute, Alain Robbe-Grillet, Michel Butor, Marguerite Duras) launched their fascinating views in such works as *Tropisms, Jealousy, Milan Passage*, and *The Square*. Although these writers did not constitute a school per se, they did share certain ideas concerning the novel. They felt that the novel was not something fixed or unalterable, but rather it was a form of expression that fluctuated with and responded to social, economic, and spiritual needs of individuals and societies. For them the novel was a kind of research project where the participants remained anonymous and progressed through their disoriented world in a Kafkaesque manner. In their novels the characters' situations are never clear-cut: they are either part of a giant megalopolis or a family in a building, or they reflect certain relationships. Their inner worlds are revealed to the reader through signs, symptoms, fleeting images, and objects.

Personalities in the works of the New Novelists are for the most part faceless, that is, the protagonists are divested of structured and unified personalities. Robbe-Grillet's circulatory detective story *The Erasers* (1953) centers the events lived out in a circumscribed period of twenty-four hours. The antihero protagonist seeks a forever-changing world about him, which the author notes with geometrical precision. Concomitantly, he is being viewed in a constantly shifting manner, through direct and indirect discourse, interior monologue, reversed chronology, flashbacks, fantasy images, and by a multitude of strangers whom he meets during the course of his peregrinations. There is, therefore, not just one concrete description of the antihero; there is not just one personality. There are as many personalities as there are observers.

Nin used the new shattering-of-the-personality technique with felicity. By perpetually altering situations and events in Sabina's life, she succeeded in giving the impression of a woman whose psyche is truly dispersed. An example of this literary device occurs at the outset of the novel, Sabina is in a Greenwich Village nightclub talking to some of her friends. The same scene is repeated with slight variations at the conclusion of the work. In both scenes Sabina is described in a number of ways by different viewers in the nightclub. She is ambiguous and mysterious. What is Sabina *really* like? How does she *really* react? Important too is that the reworking of the original image disrupts the linear structure the reader may bring to the novel. When did incidents occur? Are they the same incidents? Further disorientation or disintegration of the conventional novel and of the so-called unified personality occurs. In *Ladders to Fire* Sabina was described as "dressed in red and silver, she evoked sounds and imagery of fire engines as they tore through the streets of New York." These lines and others, such as "Only her ladder led to fire," are repeated in *A Spy in the House of Love*. Like a refrain, phrases and sentences, metaphors and images are imbricated throughout the volume, accentuating the painful periods in Sabina's life, the uneven and un-answered heartbeats that conclude each of her unsatisfactory love affairs.

In the style of the New Novelists, time and space are *dechronologized*, feelings and sensations are expressed through "undefinable inner movements," through gestures, feelings, sometimes words. Hence, characters are not able to enter and exit at will, but are brought up in conversations, reveries, dreams, hallucinations, or by proliferating objects of which they are a part. Presences, whether animate or inanimate, become catalysts, that is, active forces participat-ing in events, not just passive entities. A woman's cape spread out on a bed is transformed into "the bed of no-mads"; viewed another way, the same cape becomes "the flag of adventure." A door stands for "painful tension." "Sand" deposited on Sabina's skin on the beach is trans-muted into "muslin." Each object in its own way acts upon the protagonist emotionally and therefore physically. Ges-tures, so important to Nathalie Sarraute in revealing inner movements—those composites of images, sensations, and feelings—were likewise Nin's tool in communicating equiv-alent emotions to the reader. Sabina's husband's "deliberate gesture" when taking up her valise and putting it down with care indicates "a rock-like center to his movements, a sense of perfect gravitation." From his manner in dealing with the object, the reader knows that "his emotions, his thoughts revolved around a fixed center like a well-organized plane-tary system." The husband, then, is a conventional, good-hearted person with no imagination, no drive, no poetry. The way in which Sabina talks one evening at a bar empha- sizes her inner pulsion and her lack of identity. "She talked profusely and continuously with a feverish breathlessness, like one in fear of silence. She sat as if she could not bear to sit for long; and, when she rose to buy cigarettes, she was equally eager to return to her seat." Sabina's amoebalike nature, her ego, cut her off from her surroundings and from herself. She lives in the collective realm, a rootless and frenetic existence.

Nin wrote polyphonically, as did Michel Butor. In *Milan Passage* (1954), Butor's central image is an apart- ment house in Paris, a world in itself. The people inhabiting this microcosm and their activities are looked upon as one giant chess game: each creature is a pawn, each combina- tion an act of destiny, each entanglement a move to decide upon. It was Butor's goal to discover the secret order that reigns behind the façade, the world of reality hidden behind parallel existences. Butor proceeded to unravel the lives of the inhabitants of the apartment house by relating their conversations and activities in parallel and simultaneous sequences as though a giant orchestra and chorale were being sounded, each voice heard not as the one and only but in relationship to the entire group.

As in Butor's polyphonic structure, Sabina's conscious and unconscious activities are related in parallel and simul- taneous constructs like units on a chessboard or parts of a puzzle. But unlike Butor's cohesive whole (the apartment house), Sabina's world never comes together: "Wherever I am, I am in many pieces, not daring to bring them all together, any more than I would dare to bring the two men together. Now I am where I will not be hurt, for a few days at least I will not be hurt in any way . . . but I am not all of me here, only half of me is being sheltered." Sabina's mul- tiple selves are endlessly dismembering and reblending them- selves into new but parallel situations: her lovers are one and the same, either Don Juans verging on the homosexual or narcissistic passive creatures. Her pain is likewise re-played like a broken record: her fears of hurting her husband and others, her corrosive guilt feelings, her inability to find fulfillment.

There are so many levels to Sabina's personality that each sequence resembles a geological fold in which polyvalent combinations, clusters of despair, and torment are unraveled. As with Marguerite Duras's heroines, particularly Lol V. Stein, we are confronted with a slow-paced and quasi-detached spiritual and psychological operation: a death-rebirth ritual, an initiation during the course of which a new wholeness is hoped for but never achieved. And as with Duras's heroines, we are led down the road to further conflict, further deterioration of the ego. In each of Sabina's soliloquies, readers are introduced to a highly charged personal poetry: a complex of interwoven images, beguiling sensations and impressions, a blending of Oriental control and inwardness and Occidental ebullience and outwardness.

What is perhaps the most innovative device of all in *A Spy in the House of Love* is the creation of the Lie Detector, a machine endowed with a living quality. It is Sabina's alter ego, her conscience, which follows her at all times and torments or irritates her, but finally forces her to become aware of her fruitless activities. Taking on the characteristics of the devil's advocate, the Lie Detector relentlessly questions and objectifies, thus forcing awareness, and compels Sabina to face her actions and feelings and learn how to deal with them. The Lie Detector informs her:

There is only one relief: to confess, to be caught, tried, punished. That's the ideal of every criminal. But it's not quite so simple. Only half of the self wants to atone, to be freed of the torments of guilt. The other half of man wants to continue to be free. Soon only one half surrenders, calling out "catch me," while the other half creates obstacles, difficulties; seeks to escape.

In Sabina's case, her conscience points one way; it remains faithful to her husband. Her body, on the other hand, indi-

cates another course. As a catalyst, the Lie Detector encourages conflict, for only through opposition can both
polarities come into focus.

The Lie Detector is also an inner voice that possesses
its own tone, its own personality. A component part of Sabina's being, it forces her ear to record its message, to codify
its syntax, to espouse the least inflection of feeling, which
varies during the course of the narrative. Each nuance alters
her sensations and relationships. The Lie Detector is always
there, creating the inner havoc only a paranoid knows: "It
was not a surprise, because it was a materialization of a
feeling she had known for many years: that of an Eye
watching and following her through her life."

A Cosmic Eye, the moon, is also of great import to
Sabina. She used to love to take "moon baths," whereas
others took sun baths. People said that moon baths were
dangerous, but she evidently enjoyed the excitement and
terror of the unknown. No one knew the effect of moon
baths, "but it was intimated that it might be the opposite of
the sun's effect." The moon brings on lunacy, insanity, or an
animal-like nature—and Sabina lay naked under the light of
the moon for hours on end.

By this ritual it seemed to her that her skin acquired a different
glow, a night glow, an artificial luminousness which showed its
fullest effulgence only at night, in artificial light. . . . It accentu-
ated her love of mystery.

The moon is said to be responsible for outer disturbances
(storms, tidal waves) and also supposedly activates chaos
within the mind, arousing turmoil or generating overactivity.
The moon radiates an eerie light in darkness, dulls illumination, and reflects, thus becoming the instigator of visions and
hallucinations. The moon inspires magic, understanding,
ecstasy, and insight—the forces emanating from the darkest
and most archaic regions within beings. Sabina likewise
arouses fascination. She belongs to the group known as

Night People. Deep within her exist dark forces that have not yet been brought to life: a world of archaic impulses and instincts, still undifferentiated, still bathed in darkness.

But Sabina, activated by the moonrays, felt germinating in her the power to extend time in the ramification of myriad lives and loves, to expand the journey to infinity, taking immense and luxurious detours as the courtesan depositor of multiple desires.

In addition to her moon qualities, Sabina is a female Don Juan, a siren engulfed in the ambiguity of her nature. But whereas Don Juan considered himself above and beyond Good and Evil, therefore never experiencing guilt, Sabina is continuously tortured by remorse. She would like to be different and rise above her eroticism; yet, she thrives on sensuality and perversity. As a siren type she is thrilled to allure men. The Sirens, let us recall, half fish and half woman, were autoerotic and attracted not to one man but all men. Incapable of loving an individual, these mythological creatures knew only desire and sought to conquer men in general, attempting to gain power over them and control them. They lived in an undifferentiated realm.

Other problems also come into view. Just as Don Juan suffered from a mother complex—that is, he was a son looking for his mother in all the women he met—so Sabina has a father complex. Like many nymphomaniacs, she seeks that father image in the men with whom she has relations. Interestingly, these Don Juan figures, whether male or female, usually have finely developed Eros characteristics: they relate very well to people and display feelings of great tenderness, understanding, and insight. Sabina always is solicitous of others, the center of attraction, personable and ingratiating.

Whereas César Franck's *Symphony in D Minor* was used to interweave the polyphonies of feeling and sensation in *Children of the Albatross*, jazz is focused upon here to express Sabina's instinctual world. Her *café au lait* lover,

Mambo—whose primitive nature is revealed in the rhythm of his walk, in the syncopation of his drumbeat, and in the melodic improvisations of his songs—mesmerizes her. Sabina finds herself in another sphere of existence, deep in the jazz culture; gone is the guilt-filled puritanical world. Important to her is the soloist as well as the entire body of instruments and combinations, each in its way adding texture to her feelings, boldness to her venture. Her Mambo seems to encompass all the Louis Armstrongs, Buddu Boldens, Duke Ellingtons, Fats Wallers. Although an individual, Mambo is an archetypal figure, a black divinity whose powerful harmonies and cacophonies, beats and syncopations, capture her entire being.

Despite all of her lovers, the Lie Detector tells her, she has not yet loved.

You've been trying to love, beginning to love. Trust alone is not love, desire alone is not love, illusion is not love, dreaming is not love. All these were paths leading you out of yourself, it is true, and so you thought they led to another, but you never reached the other. You were only on the way.

Compassion marks the Lie Detector's voice in his attempt to reassure Sabina; by the same token, he asks her to face herself. Sabina begins to cry, and her tears have a curative effect. They are a baptism into a new sphere of being, a fresh beginning. To express the quintessence of her emotions, Nin has Sabina listen to a Beethoven quartet. It is in chamber music, Nin believed, that Beethoven's depth of inspiration and purity of feeling are most fully expressed; it is here that the contemplative inner life rather than the spectacular outer world is illuminated. Sabina experiences a coalescing of her chaotic inner pulsions and with it "a complete dissolution of the eyes, gestures, as if she were losing her essence." The Lie Detector extends his hands "as if to rescue her." For the first time, perhaps, Sabina begins to understand the polarities that pull at her, stridently and abrasively.

Solar Barque/Seduction of the Minotaur

Cities of the Interior concludes with *Solar Barque* and *Seduction of the Minotaur*, a two-part novel in which Lilian pursues her worldly adventure. In Part I, *Solar Barque*, Lilian is the actress. She experiences events and people, effulgences and velleities of life. In Part II, *Seduction of the Minotaur*, she objectifies her activities, analyzes them, and comes to terms with their positive and negative effects. The birth of new awareness and a distillation of heretofore conflicting polarities creates the new Lilian. It is not by chance that she recalls the Talmudic words: "We do not see things as they are, we see them as we are" (*Seduction*, p. 16). Her task is to activate her discerning faculties, to allow herself to see into her "cities of the interior" so that she will neither be blinded by the radiance of an emotional relationship nor wounded by its cutting edges. Nin wrote that in *Solar Barque* and in *Seduction of the Minotaur*, she "finally succeeded in absorbing the interpretations, the knowledge, the vision of the analyst within the novelist."

The action of *Solar Barque* takes place in Golconda, Mexico, where the sun "painted everything with gold." We learn in a flashback that after renouncing Jay, Lilian returned to her husband, Larry, and her children; but when she realized the situation was unsatisfactory, she left for Mexico, where she now plays with a jazz orchestra in a hotel. Sunlight, radiance, and excitement act as the framework for Lilian's exotic excursion into the unknown. Like the heroes of Camus's *Weddings* and Gide's *The Fruits of the Earth*, she lives the languid life of sensuality in a drug-filled realm where oblivion is confused with freedom. Dr. Hernandez, who devotes his time to healing the sick and suffers from an unfortunate marital situation (a wife who wants to remain in the capital and refuses to share in his altruistic activities), becomes Lilian's confidant. It is he who explains the true meaning of psychological karma to her. Her present chaotic state is a reenactment of some unresolved conflict in her past: "You are a fugitive from truth." Escape is no longer possible.

Another friend, Hatcher, an American engineer who dresses and tries to act like a native Mexican, remains anchored in his needs. At home he has everything civilization has to offer: medicines, canned foods, clothes, and more. Lilian wonders whether he loves his new wife "with her oily black hair, her maternal body" or is it another artifice he set in his path toward escape? Then Dr. Hernandez is ambushed by drug addicts and killed. Alone now, Lilian ponders over his words, "The design comes from within." It is her task to understand herself, to sound herself out.

The Seduction of the Minotaur begins as Lilian is "journeying homeward." No more is she to escape from her acts. Relationships are going to be examined with precision and depth as she seeks out the minotaur in her labyrinth, that factor within her she fears will devour her. She finally encounters the monster within and, like the mystics of old, breaks down the protective walls of artifice she has erected throughout the years. In so doing, she unites the Dionysian and Apollonian polarities of her personality. She begins to understand her husband's various attitudes toward his work, children, and her. She sees an evolution in her thought processes and in her emotional reactions. Not any more exclusively masochistic or maternal, attempting to satisfy her inner hungers in general (integrate the polarities within her being), Lilian has become *whole*: solar and lunar barques unite.

"An archaeology of the soul," *Solar Barque* and *Seduction of the Minotaur* reflect a quest by the author, to use Michel Butor's expression, "the apprehension of reality."[18] As Butor in his novels, from *Milan Passage* to *Degrees*, sought to discover the true man, the *real* things, and a correspondence between form and structure, so Nin searches for a new blending between people, things, and the world in which they live. For Nin and for Butor, exploration therefore is not only limited to the human sphere, it includes the concrete and temporal world as well. An alliance with music, for example, is "mutually enlightening" for both man and his invention. Space is examined by Butor and by Nin as if through the lenses of a camera: each area is evoked separately, as if the author were taking a picture; its composition, perspectives, color, and form are all taken into consideration before snapping the shutter closed. As in trick photography, however, new images are superimposed on the first image, thus expanding its meaning, blurring its contours, and creating new spatiality. As the musician "projects his composition into the space of his lined paper," so the novelist "disposes of different individual histories" in his work, orchestrating all of nature, visible and invisible, in one *whole* volume—with volume.[19]

The solar barque is guided by the sun principle. It seeks organic warmth. In this trajectory, Lilian's libido flows outward into the sun-drenched land of Mexico. There she lives viscerally as a jazz player and within the framework of nature.

According to Egyptian iconography, the dead descended in their boat to twelve inferior regions, marked with all kinds of dangers, among them serpents and demons. If the bark were strong enough and sufficiently well equipped, it advanced in its subterranean journey until it reached its final resting place: the clarity of light. In *Solar Barque* Lilian undertakes a similarly perilous journey. In the dazzling Mexican sun she must undergo her first initiation and experience the light of reason: her relationships must be no longer clandestine, but rather lived out for all to see. Every event in which she participates and every person she meets acts as an illuminating force, a catalyst, in her progressive awakening of consciousness. Like the Argonauts and Ulysses, she en-

counters dangers and gets caught up in adventures. A victim
of her own Siren-like nature, she may lose her course; thus
she must protect herself from "promiscuity" (p. 107).

Light, associated throughout *Solar Barque* with gold,
the purest of metals and noblest of states, entices Lilian
through the perils of illumination. It is in this brilliantly lit
atmosphere that she experiences a kind of epiphany. She
knows now escape is not for her. There is no escape into
darkness in her brilliant sunlight; the solar rays do not dim.
But there is the danger of blindness that may result from too
lengthy an immersion in the physical world. There is also
the danger of her moist inner world drying up if she keeps
floating about "on a celestial ocean," if the light of reason
continually dominates. Nevertheless, Lilian makes her way
into the Mexican world and with the aid of the new light
sees into the traps and pitfalls of life. She learns to experience "the sea's aluminum reflectors" and "the lagoon on the
left of the road" that "showed a silver surface" (p. 9). Lilian
no longer experiences guilt or masochism. She has to make
the "intense indigoes" and "the flaming oranges . . . ," "the
flesh tones of pomegranates" part of her world; then interweave these burning emotions into her psyche, thus remov-
ing their power over her.

Every inner exploration in this land of fire is "full of
burning life," whether it is "the radium shafts of the sea" (p.
49), or the heavens that "took fire" and became like "lami-
nated coral," or the water resembling a "pool of mercury, so
iridescent, so clinging" (p. 50). Lilian has absorbed herself
in nature and become one with the cosmos. Instead of hear-
ing only the guitars, she now hears "the music of the body,"
nature's rhythms, in observing scenes such as women walking, lifting water jugs on their heads, or shepherds tending
their flock. Nature's power over her has become dominant,
absorbing. For a time, Lilian experiences depersonalization
and dehumanization—a blending directly into the collective
sphere—like the initiate who divests himself on his mortal
self to experience the God within. She is able now to per-

ceive the meaning of the "expanse of sky" and likens it to "an infinite canvas on which human beings were incapable of projecting images from their human life because they would seem out of scale and absurd" (p. 15).

Listening to the pounding of the sea, Lilian hears not only one instrument but an orchestration of sounds, colors, and feelings: "The waves, attracted by the music, would unroll like a bolt of silk . . ." (p. 51). Lilian feels the interrelatedness of phenomena, the permutations necessary to travel from the world of sense perception to the nonperceptual continuum existing outside of the visual and temporal space/time concept.

Words had no weight. The intensity of the colors made them float in space like balloons, and the velvet texture of the climate gave them a purely decorative quality like other flowers. They had no abstract meaning, being received by the senses. (p. 16)

Sonorities, syntheses, inversions, antitheses, and repetitions are only a few of the literary devices used by Nin to set up an ever-widening pattern within the text, thus arousing infinite sympathetic vibrations in the protagonists as well as in the reader and, in so doing, expanding consciousness.

With the aid of the two father images, Dr. Hernandez and Hatcher, Lilian learns to distinguish between reality and artificiality—that is, between objects inhabiting her inner world and objects that lie outside of her unconscious spatiality. Dr. Hernandez, a sacrificial agent, is a positive father figure. He helps Lilian pursue her initiation into her own unconscious—a potential world where she will experience destruction and rebirth. Hatcher, a negative father figure, represents the man who seeks to escape from life, unable to face his many selves, and wearing a veil over his eyes, thus living peripherally.

As is generally true of sacrificial figures (e.g., Moses, Christ), Dr. Hernandez must die before his mission is complete. It is for his followers to see to the completion of his life's goal. Like the Lie Detector in *A Spy in the House of*

Love, Dr. Hernandez emphasizes the words "remembering" and "forgetting"—the double-life process, the pattern each individual sets for himself: "And one day we open our eyes, and there we are caught in the same pattern, repeating the same story. How could it be otherwise? The design comes from within us. It is eternal" (p. 19). He wants to illuminate Lilian and show her how one must penetrate into "the mysteries of the human labyrinth from which she was a fugitive." At times Lilian grows angry at his persistent probing; at other times, she withdraws. But he persists.

Lilian returns again and again to the notion of the labyrinth. In ancient Egypt, Crete, Lemnos, Etruria, they were structures with mazelike networks of passageways, and abysses, whirlpools, reproducing for some complex celestial patterns, for others inner chaos. Within the labyrinth one may lose one's way or one may reach what mystics call the *Center*. From the Center one becomes able to reconstruct one's life by working one's way out of the maze into daylight —emerging with new understanding and greater balance.

During one of Lilian's conversations with Dr. Hernandez, they sit in a "hand-carved canoe," an object that has great significance for both: it is a presence that mirrors their own life journey. The canoe is not depersonalized; on the contrary, "the human hand on the knife had made uneven indentations of the scooped-out tree trunk which caught the light like the scallops of the sea shell" (p. 21). The image of the water, mountains, and sun is compared to an "impressionist painting" (p. 21). It preserves the intensity of the colors but replicates them in a subjective way, the outer world affected by the senses. Artists such as Monet, Sisley, and Pissarro had allowed color to return to its purity, "to vibrate" with its "natural intensity."[20] Lilian's impressionism, like that of the painters of this school, allows her to experience form and movement. It gives her (so alienated an individual) some kind of stability, some human sanction that makes her aware of her own existence as well as of objective reality. Lilian and Dr. Hernandez continue their "flowing journey" on their solar barque; their pattern is circular, as though they are rounding the earth, embracing the sun disk, experiencing Being and Oneness, which are the energy implicit in the Indian and Tibetan mandalas and which exist within the universe of variables and contingencies.

Hatcher, in contrast, is "an echo from the past" (p. 75). He reminds Lilian of her father, perhaps because Hatchet is blind to his own foibles. "Like her father he was always commanding" and his "smile too was a quarter-tone smile, as if he had no time to radiate, to expand" (p. 75). Hatcher is so interested in "affirming his happiness" that Lilian realizes he is really a miserable creature. He cannot remain still and is not contemplative, but always budding, shifting, going about everywhere at a frenetic pace.

Filled with bitterness against his first wife and against America, Hatcher is a man at odds with himself, solitary in his world, chaotic in his essence, and unformed, yet rich with possibilities. As Lilian observes him, she finds herself returning to her own world of silence, into meditation and contemplation. She does not reject the chaos condition in herself; on the contrary, she incorporates it within her inner world.

Seduction of the Minotaur revolves around Lilian's journey homeward to New York City and her family. The moon rather than the solar image predominates now. The moon reflects light, it does not generate it. The moon is the symbol of transformation and growth; it follows biological rhythms and submits to the universal law of becoming. The moon represents nocturnal values, the unconscious; thus it represents Lilian's evolution, change in pattern, direction, and indirection.

During her homeward lunar journey Lilian is going to experience awareness and penetrate her labyrinthine, cave-like areas alone and unaided. Strengthened by Dr. Hernandez's gentle ways, his positive and understanding attitude,

Lilian contemplates the multiplicity of her world. Such a meditative attitude helps her develop matriarchal consciousness, which "characterizes the spiritual nature of woman."[21] Heretofore Lilian has lived viscerally, for the moment, attempting always to escape from a present reality into an "infantile" land of enchantment, living through one ecstatic interlude after another, through one joy after another. Her desperate need to escape from her own nature, corroded with guilt, fear, shame, and pain, had once marked Lilian's course. Now, however, the moon spirit, related to measured attitudes, meditation, memory, meaning, and dreams, is being activated.

Lilian's personality is reflected in her attitude toward music. Before her trip to Mexico she had "abandoned classical music and had become a jazz pianist. Classical music could not contain her improvisations, her tempo, her vehemences" (p. 115). Lilian has lived according to the quantitative time scheme of patriarchal consciousness: from one extreme to another and with no power of evaluation. Now she alters the situation and lives qualitatively, expressing her being, whether favorably or not, to be herself as she truly is.

Matriarchal consciousness, which Lilian is now developing, helps her relate to reality. Her heart and her head will speak to her. To the ancient Egyptian, the heart was "the original source of thought and of the creative spirit." In India, the heart was associated with the moon; it combined psyche and body. The heart, or the Center, gives Lilian the orientation and balance she needs to understand her own creative spirit, her longing for independence, not at the exclusion of the real world and real people—namely, her family—but including them. What Lilian brings back to New York is not a series of souvenirs or objects, "but the softness of the atmosphere, the tenderness of the voices, the caressing colors and the whispering presence of an underworld of memory" (p. 95). She is less rebellious now. Her "inner turmoil" has quieted. She is receptive to her husband and children and to their labyrinths.

Growth needs "stillness and invisibility, not loudness and light." It is therefore during the second part of her trajectory, the moon phase, that Lilian is able to experience the memory and reflection, the fullness of the radiant sun. Now the rays allow the seed to germinate within her, the plant to gestate. Daytime is not the period for procreation; night is. And there must also be solitude, secrecy, and concealment. The "Moon is lord of life and growth, in opposition to the lethal devouring sun."[22] The night is moist. Sleep allows the healing process to go on; it allows the individual to recollect and recover memories in the limitless dimensions of his unconscious. In Babylonian mythology, the moon, Sin, is a physician who cures at night in secret and in veiled ways. It is not by chance that Dr. Hernandez is a healing figure for Lilian. Although abraded by his radiance during his lifetime, his power after death generates an inner light and organic warmth for her. As Lilian sinks into the quiescence of her moon world, the life energy he has injected into her through their lengthy walks activates her own libido that now can flow into others and back into herself, a double process that will help her consciously orient and adapt to the world of multiplicity and cope with her own frustrations.

Lilian's instincts have been filtered, the veil lifted. She now sees sharply into herself. The Dionysian and Apollonian sides of her personality are sharply etched, as powerfully as the double ax, symbol of the Cretan labyrinth with its Minotaur at the Center. This monstrous being, bearing the head of a man and the body of a bull, extracted his bounty every seven years in the form of seven Athenian youths and maidens. It must be noted in connection with this legend that the Creto-Mycenaean culture was a patriarchate in its earliest days. It was transformed into a matriarchate where the Great Mother archetype prevailed. It was the Great Mother who sent the "Aphrodite mania," which consisted of sexuality and hysteria, to her enemies. These obsessions, frequently repressed or dormant, as they are in the beginning of the Phaedra myth, surge forth with all of their power in time. Like Phaedra, Lilian at the outset of her journey was a "psychic fragmentation" and a victim of the Great Mother archetype. Unlike Phaedra, though, Lilian is able to face the Minotaur within her. "It was not a monster. It was a reflection upon a mirror, a masked woman, Lilian herself, the hidden masked part of herself unknown to her, who had ruled her acts. She extended her hand toward this tyrant who could no longer harm her (p. 111).

Lilian has come a long way. She has found and established contact with the animal within her, the instinctual Dionysian realm. She has also understood the Apollonian, or the rational, aspect of life. Her need to be someone else and to escape from herself has vanished. Her expanded consciousness allows her to unify what was disparate.

Conclusion

Nin's works are visualizations of an inner necessity, a truth shaped and fashioned into art form. Jakob Burckhardt wrote in *Reflections on History*: ". . . without art we should not know that truth exists, for truth is only made visible, apprehensible and acceptable in the work of art."[1] Thought, feeling, and dream are caught up in metaphors, images, alliterations—infrared lights that hurtle, cut, and bruise protagonists and reader like "stalactite torches" or lull them into a state of receptivity. Nin's writings interweave the visual and the aural into complex universal designs. Reader and protagonist converge, as do viewer and painting in an art gallery, in preparation for a physical and mental involvement.

Nin's novels and short stories are alchemical and force transmutation, altering matter and spirit. Like the alchemist, who labored in silence and seclusion, projecting his inner world onto the elements with which he was working, Nin personifies her sensations and endows them with all types of human and animal characteristics. Similar to the alchemical process, activity in Nin's novels and short stories encourages a dual process: like a warm uterus it nurtures; yet paradoxically it stifles. Motion frequently becomes stilled, feelings imprisoned, and sequences nonexistent. Time freezes. Space congeals. The reader then makes his way into the instinctual domain, which becomes activated. The single creative act is fomented; germination occurs. Subject and object fuse in muted tones as an unsettling emotional condition pervades. In Nin's secret world of analogy, primordial vibrations are sounded in silence like a heaving heart. They create a visceral response in the reader and set up an empathetic state— a "feeling into"—but the depth of the attachment depends upon the power of the reader's projection.

For Nin, perception was a vital process in her writing. It is controlled instinct, multidirectional and arbitrary, she suggested, and awakens confused sensations. Her visual world, whether describing a chess game, a houseboat, a Greenwich Village café, a snow storm, or exotic Mexican greenery, is not representational. It does not delineate the physical space of a Renaissance painting; rather, it brings to life a spiritual and emotional area as concretized in the statues and paintings of modern times. She has banished from view the three-dimensional picture space that prolongs the reader's reality. Her space bathes in dimensionless tonal values and a series of transparencies. Her visual image provokes a synchronistic condition. It inhabits a space/time continuum where reader and protagonists are static as well as mobile. The world of the mystic now comes into being, the eternal present, the experience of *Bardo*, which Nin said she *knew* during the creative process, a world of transcendence, "that intermediate state between death and rebirth"— the void from which creation arises.

Because Nin was more sensitive than the ordinary individual, because she had suffered so acutely after her father's desertion and knew years of solitude and loneliness, the struggle to achieve her rightful place as woman and artist had been arduous. She carved her way unflaggingly. Neither passive nor restive, she realized that toil and perseverance were important factors in the making of the artist. She confronted her inner world, and in this inexpressible sphere she came to know "the obscure feelings" that make for the solemn and the grandiose—the world beyond appearances, the *mysterium tremendum*. Her descent into self as artist and woman enabled her to confront her impulses, to perceive cataclysms, and to foresee abysses. Endowed with the magical powers of the creative individual—or with divine force—her feelings and instincts paralleled and fused with the visual experience.

The image was a symbol for Nin—the visible sign of a transcendental reality. It must not be analyzed too explicitly, she believed. To do so would be to deprive the image of its mystery, to divest it of the elements that arouse the creative impulse within the artist. Spinoza declared in his *Ethics* that as soon as an idea emerges into clarity and becomes overly rational, emotion ceases to be emotion. Let us recall that Nin took umbrage at Dr. Allendy's psychoanalytical method for the same reason: it was ultra-scientific, ultra-rationalistic, ultra-circumscribed—ultra-sterile. For Nin and for Dr. Otto Rank, the symbol became a "psychic transformer;" it rendered visible what lay hidden in Nin's depths. As long as it was not impoverished by the light of reason, this catalyst remained fertile. It stirred, activated, and irritated the energy that revivified the symbol, making hers the eternal world of birth and rebirth.

Nin the woman and artist, the lecturer and essayist, influenced young and old alike. Her *Diary*, her critical and conceptual works—*D. H. Lawrence: An Unprofessional Study, The Novel of the Future, Realism and Reality*— indicated the way as well as explored and explained techniques and conventions implicit in the writing of novels: uses of images, phrases, tonalities, character delineations, how reality may be transmuted, sensations decanted, and feelings crystallized in the work of art. Encouraging the talented, instilling confidence in the timid, suggesting inner probings to those who feared a descent into self, Nin was always available to the emotionally and spiritually needy. With dignity, sensitivity, extreme understanding, and love, she enlightened the groping, succored the falling, and aided the faceless in seeking their own way. For many, Nin played the role of the positive mother archetype; for others, she was an *anima* figure—a *femme inspiratrice*, sister and bride.

Nin never envisaged life without pain or creation without struggle. She agreed with D. H. Lawrence's dictum as stated in his Foreword to *Women in Love*:

Man struggles with his unborn needs and fulfilment. New unfoldings struggle up in torment in him, as buds struggle forth from the midst of a plant. Any man of real individuality tries to know and to understand what is happening, even in himself, as he goes along. This struggle for verbal consciousness should not be left out in art. It is a very great part of life. It is not superimposition of a theory. It is the passionate struggle into conscious being.

The interplay of the powerful forces within Nin molded her into a woman of inner and outer beauty who danced, laughed, sighed, wept, breathed as she stilled the flowing, limited the infinite, personified the amorphous, and decanted her images in structured feelings and translucent arabesques. Love and joy, like nacre, lined her being.

Notes

Introduction

1. Anaïs Nin, *In Favor of the Sensitive Man*, p. 31.
2. Anaïs Nin, unpublished letter to the author, n.d.
3. Nin, unpublished letter to the author, March 10, 1970.

2. Creative Criticism

1. E. D. Hirsch, Jr., "Literary Evaluation as Knowledge." In L. S. Dembo, *Criticism*, p. 49.
2. D. H. Lawrence, *Studies in Classic American Literature* p. 67.
3. Albert Einstein, *Out of My Later Years*, p. 260.
4. See Evelyn J. Hinz, "The Beginning and the End: Lawrence's *Psychoanalysis* and *Fantasie*," *Dalhousie Review* LII (Summer, 1972), pp. 251–65.
5. Quoted by Keith Alldritt, *The Visual Imagination of D. H. Lawrence*, p. 48.
6. *Ibid.*, p. 210.
7. Serge Hutin, *Sociétés secrètes*, p. 19.
8. C. G. Jung, *Psychological Types*, p. 605.

3. *House of Incest*

1. Anaïs Nin, *A Woman Speaks*, ed. by Evelyn J. Hinz, p. 207.
2. André Breton, *Manifeste du surréalisme*, p. 42.

3. *Ibid.*, p. 64.
4. Franz Alexander and Sheldon T. Selesnick, *The History of Psychiatry*, pp. 170–73.
5. *Ibid.*, p. 174.
6. *Ibid.*, p. 194.
7. Anaïs Nin, *The Novel of the Future*, p. 152.
8. Anaïs Nin, *The Diary of Anaïs Nin (1931–1934)*, p. 75.
9. *Ibid.*, p. 77.
10. *Ibid.*, p. 163.
11. *Ibid.*, p. 283.
12. Jessie Taft, *Otto Rank*, p. 273.
13. Nin, *Diary (1931–1934)*, p. 270.
14. Otto Rank, *The Myth of the Birth of the Hero*, p. 293.
15. *Ibid.*, pp. 138–40.
16. *Ibid.*, p. 175.
17. Nin, *Diary (1931–1934)*, p. 185.
18. *Ibid.*, p. 271.
19. *Ibid.*, p. 276.
20. *Ibid.*, p. 286.
21. *Ibid.*, p. 265.
22. This discussion is based on my article in "The World of Anaïs Nin," *Mosaic*, ed. by Evelyn J. Hinz.
23. Nin, *Diary (1931–1934)*, p. 315.
24. Edward Edinger, "Outline of Analytical Psychology" (unpublished), p. 10.
25. Nin, *Novel of the Future*, p. 71.
26. Esther Harding, *The Way of All Women*, p. 94.
27. Edward Edinger, *Ego and Archetype*, pp. 161–62.
28. Murray Stein, "Narcissus," *Spring* (1976), pp. 38–42.
29. C. G. Jung, *Collected Works*, vol. 8, pp. 241 ff.
30. Stein, "Narcissus," p. 38.
31. *Ibid.*, p. 49.
32. John Layard, *The Virgin Archetype*, p. 281.
33. Jung, *Collected Works*, vol. 16, p. 218.
34. C. G. Jung, "Mysterium Coniunctionis," in *Collected Works*, vol. 14, p. 150.
35. Layard, *Archetype*, p. 303.
36. Gerhard Adler, *The Living Symbol*, p. 213.
37. *Ibid.*, p. 216.
38. Gaston Bachelard, *L'eau et les rêves*, p. 9.

39.   Henry Miller, "Letters to Anaïs Nin," *Southern Review*, VI
      (Spring 1970), p. 125.

4.   Antinovelettes

1.   *Winter of Artifice* was published by Dutton in 1948 and
     included two parts, "Djuna" and "The Voice." When first
     printed by Obelisk Press in 1939, it included only "Djuna."
     The Swallow Press publication (1961), to which we refer in
     this chapter, presented "collected novelettes" and included
     Stella, Winter of Artifice, and *The Voice*.
2.   Anaïs Nin, *The Diary of Anaïs Nin (1931–1934)*, p. 260.
3.   Nin, *The Diary (1939–1944)*, p. 247.
4.   Anaïs Nin, *The Novel of the Future*, p. 119.
5.   Nin, *Novel of the Future*, p. 71.
6.   C. G. Jung, *Psychological Types*, p. 593.
7.   Raphael Patai, *The Hebrew Goddess*, p. 207.

5.   A Renaissance Artist

1.   Oliver Evans, *Anaïs Nin*, p. 89.
2.   Anaïs Nin, *The Novel of the Future*, p. 74.
3.   Evelyn Hinz, *The Mirror of the Garden*, p. 51. A descrip-
     tion of the characters in terms of the four humors/elements
     is given.
4.   Nin, *Novel of the Future*, p. 24.
5.   None of the quotations from *Ladders to Fire*, published by
     Allan Swallow (1959), carries a page number. This edition,
     with line engravings by Ian Hugo, is unnumbered.
6.   Evans, *Nin*, p. 91 (unpublished lecture of Anaïs Nin).
7.   Anaïs Nin, "Stella," in *Winter of Artifice*, p. 44.
8.   Herbert Read, *A Concise History of Modern Painting*, p. 91.
9.   Evelyn J. Hinz, ed., *A Woman Speaks*, by Anaïs Nin, p. 112.
10. Nin, *Novel of the Future*, p. 108.
11. Read, *Modern Painting*, p. 121.
12. James T. Soby, *Joan Miró*, p. 39.
13. Aaron Copland, *The New Music*, p. 34.
14. Sheldon Cheney, *The Theatre*, p. 78.

15. Walter Allen, *The Modern Novel*, pp. 132–37.
16. Michel Butor, *Pour un nouveau roman*, p. 71.
17. Read, *Modern Painting*, pp. 110–117.
18. Michel Butor, *Essais sur le roman*, p. 4.
19. *Ibid.*, p. 56.
20. Read, *Modern Painting*, pp. 14–20.
21. Erich Neumann, "On the Moon and Matriarchal Consciousness," in *Dynamic Aspects of the Psyche*, pp. 50–72.
22. *Ibid.*, p. 70.

Conclusion

1. Herbert Read, *Art and Alienation*, p. 21.

Bibliography

1. Works by Anaïs Nin

D. H. Lawrence: An Unprofessional Study. Paris: Edward W. Titus, 1932.

The House of Incest. Paris: Siana Editions, 1936. Reprint. Denver: Alan Swallow, 1958. Photo-Montages by Val Telberg.

Winter of Artifice. Paris: The Obelisk Press, 1939. Reprint. Denver: Alan Swallow, 1961. Engravings by Ian Hugo.

Under a Glass Bell. New York: Gemor Press, 1944. Reprint. Denver: Alan Swallow, 1966. Engravings by Ian Hugo.

Realism and Reality. New York: Alicat Book Shop, 1946.

Children of the Albatross. New York: E. P. Dutton, 1947. Reprint. Denver: Alan Swallow, 1966.

On Writing. Hanover, New Hampshire: Daniel Oliver Associates, 1947.

The Four-Chambered Heart. New York: Duell, Sloan and Pearce, 1950. Reprint. Denver: Alan Swallow, 1966.

A Spy in the House of Love. New York: British Book Centre, 1954. Reprint. Denver: Alan Swallow, 1966.

Solar Barque. Edwards Brothers, 1958. Illustrations by Peter Loomer.

Cities of the Interior. Denver: Alan Swallow, 1959. Engravings by Ian Hugo.

Seduction of the Minotaur. Denver: Alan Swallow, 1961.

Collages. Denver: Alan Swallow, 1964.

The Diary of Anaïs Nin (1931–1934). New York: Harcourt, Brace & World, 1966.

The Diary of Anaïs Nin (1934–1939). New York: Harcourt, Brace & World, 1967.

The Novel of the Future. New York: The Macmillan Co., 1968.

The Diary of Anaïs Nin (1939–1944). New York: Harcourt, Brace & World, 1971.

The Diary of Anaïs Nin (1944–1947). New York: Harcourt Brace Jovanovich, 1971.

The Diary of Anaïs Nin (1947–1955). New York: Harcourt Brace Jovanovich, 1974.

The Diary of Anaïs Nin (1955–1966). New York: Harcourt Brace Jovanovich, 1976.

A Woman Speaks: The Lectures, Seminars and Interviews of Anaïs Nin. Edited by Evelyn J. Hinz. Chicago: Swallow Press, 1975.

In Favor of the Sensitive Man, and Other Essays. New York: Harcourt Brace Jovanovich, 1976.

Delta of Venus: Erotica. New York: Harcourt Brace Jovanovich, 1977.

Waste of Timelessness, and Other Early Stories. New York: Magic Circle Press, 1977.

Linotte. New York: Harcourt Brace Jovanovich, 1978.

The Diary of Anaïs Nin (1966–1977). New York: Harcourt Brace Jovanovich, in preparation.

2. Works on Anaïs Nin

Brodin, Pierre. *Présences contemporaines ecrivains américains d'aujourd'hui*. Paris: Nouvelles Editions Debresse, 1964.

Burford, William. *The Art of Anaïs Nin*. New York: The Alicat Bookshop, 1947.

Centing, Richard. "Under the Sign of Pisces: Anaïs Nin and Her Circle." *The Nin Newsletter*. Edited by Richard Centing and Benjamin Franklin V.

Evans, Oliver. *Anaïs Nin*. Carbondale, Illinois: Southern Illinois University Press, 1968.

Friedman, Melvin J. "André Malraux and Anaïs Nin." *Contemporary Literature* II (Winter, 1970).

Harms, Valerie, Ed. *Celebration with Anaïs Nin*. New York: Magic Circle Press, 1973.

Hinz, Evelyn J. *The Mirror and the Garden*. New York: Harcourt Brace Jovanovich, 1971, 1973.

Hinz, Evelyn J., Ed. "The World of Anaïs Nin." With an Introduction. *Mosaic* (Winter, 1978).

Kuntz, Paul G. "Art as Public Dream: The Practice and Theory of Anaïs Nin." *Journal of Aesthetics*, CXXXII (1974).

McEvilly, Wayne. "The Bread of Tradition: Reflections of the Diary of Anaïs Nin." *Prairie Schooner* XLV (1971).

Miller, Henry. "Of Art and the Future." In *Sunday after the War*. New York: New Directions, 1944.

———. "Letter to Anaïs Nin Regarding One of Her Books." In *Sunday after the War*. New York: New Directions, 1944.

———. "Un etre etoilique." In *The Cosmological Eye*. New York: New Directions, 1939.

———. "Letters to Anaïs Nin." *Southern Review* VI (Spring, 1970).

Shapiro, Karl. "The Charmed Circle of Anaïs Nin." *Book Week* (May 1, 1966).

Spencer, Sharon. *Collage of Dreams*. Chicago: The Swallow Press Inc., 1977.

Trilling, Diana. "Fiction in Review." *Nation* (January 26, 1946).

Young, Marguerite. "Marguerite Young on Anaïs Nin." *Voyages* (Fall, 1967).

Young, Vernon. "Five Novels, Three Sexes, and Death." *Hudson Review* I, No. 3.

Zaller, Robert, Ed. *A Casebook on Anaïs Nin*. New York: New American Library, 1974.

3. Secondary Sources

Adler, Gerhard. *The Living Symbol*. New York: Pantheon, 1961.

Alldritt, Keith. *The Visual Imagination of D. H. Lawrence*. London: Edward Arnold, 1971.

Allen, Walter. *The Modern Novel*. New York: Dutton and Co., 1965.

Alexander, Franz, and Selesnick, Sheldon T. *The History of Psychiatry*. New York: Harper and Row, 1966.

Bachelard, Gaston. *L'eau et les rêves*. Paris: José Corti, 1942.

Butor, Michel. *Pour un nouveau roman*. Paris: Gallimard, 1963.

———. *Essais sur le roman*. Paris: Gallimard, 1964.

Breton, André. *Manifeste du surréalisme*. Paris: Gallimard, 1963.

Edinger, Edward. "Outline of Analytical Psychology." Unpublished.

Edinger, Edward, *Ego and Archetype*. New York: Putnam, 1972.

Einstein, Albert. *Out of My Later Years*. New York: Philosophical Library, 1950.

Copland, Aaron. *The New Music*. New York: Norton and Co., 1969.

Cheney, Sheldon. *The Theatre*. New York: Tudor Publishing Co., 1947.

Harding, Esther. *The Way of All Women*. New York: Harper and Row, 1975.

Hirsch, E. D., Jr. "Literary Evaluation as Knowledge." In L. S. Dembo. *Criticism*. Madison: University of Wisconsin Press, 1968.

Hutin, Serge. *Sociétés secrètes*. Paris: Press universitaires de France, 1970.

Jung, C. G. *Psychological Types*. New York: Pantheon Books, 1964.

———. *Memories, Dreams, Reflections*. New York: Pantheon Books, 1963.

———. *Collected Works*, Volume 8. Princeton: Princeton University Press, 1969.

———. *Collected Works*, Volume 14. New York: Pantheon Books, 1963.

———. *Collected Works*, Volume 16. New York: Pantheon Books, 1966.

Kirk, G. S., and Raven, M. E. *The Presocratic Philosophers*. Cambridge: At the University Press, 1957.

Kuh, Katherine. *Modern Art Explained*. London: Cory, Adams and Mackay, 1965.

Layard, John. *The Virgin Archetype*. Zurich: Spring Publications, 1972.

Moynahan, Julian. *The Deed of Life*. Princeton: Princeton University Press, 1963.

Neumann, Erich. "On the Moon and Matriarchal Consciousness." In *Dynamic Aspects of the Psyche*. New York: New York Analytical Psychology Club, 1955.

Patai, Raphael. *The Hebrew Goddess*. New York: Ktav, 1967.

Rank, Otto. *Art and Artist.* New York: Tudor Publishing Co., 1932.

————. *The Myth of the Birth of the Hero, and Other Writings.* New York: Vintage Books, 1964.

Read, Herbert. *A Concise History of Modern Painting.* New York: Frederick A. Praeger, 1959.

————. *Art and Alienation.* New York: The Viking Press, 1970.

Rubin, William S. *Surrealism.* New York: Museum of Modern Art, 1968.

Soby, James T. *Joan Miró.* New York: Doubleday and Co., 1959.

Stein, Murray. "Narcissus." *Spring* (1976).

Taft, Jessie. *Otto Rank.* New York: Julian Press, 1958.

Tedlock, E. W., Jr. *D. H. Lawrence: Artist and Rebel.* Albuquerque: University of New Mexico Press, 1965.

Index